PATHWAYS

To the Science Standards

Middle School Edition

Editor
Steven J. Rakow

Guidelines for Moving the Vision into Practice

NSTA Pathways to the Science Standards:
Guidelines for Moving the Vision into Practice

MIDDLE SCHOOL EDITION

Editor: Steven J. Rakow

Contributing Editors: Juliana Texley, Karen Reynolds, Lawrence F. Lowery, Sheila Marshall

Contributors: Hans O. Anderson, Rodger Bybee, Mike Clough, Michael DiSpezio, Jo Dodds, Shelley Fisher, Gerald Foster, Linda Froschauer, Jennifer Grogg, Katherine Hilts, Page Keeley, Dave Kennedy, Melinda Mills, Karen Ostlund, Michael Padilla, Gerald Skoog, John Staver, Dana Van Burgh, Pat Warren, Carol Williams, NSTA Middle Level Standing Committee

Contributors to the Facilities Appendix: James Biehle, LaMoine Motz, Victor Showalter, Sandra West, Editor: Suzanne Lieblich

NSTA Project Manager: Sheila Marshall
NSTA Editorial Assistants: Anne Burns, Cara Young
Production Manager: Catherine Lorrain-Hale

NSTA is grateful for the generous contributions by the funders that made this effort possible:
Monsanto Fund
DuPont
American Petroleum Institute
Chemical Manufacturers Association

NSTA would like to thank the National Research Council of the National Academy of Sciences for permission to reprint material that originally appeared in the National Science Education Standards **(Washington, DC: National Academy Press, © 1996)**

Gerald Wheeler, NSTA Executive Director
Phyllis Marcuccio, NSTA Associate Executive Director
Marily DeWall, NSTA Associate Executive Director

Cover: Elinor Allen, Allen and Associates, Ltd. Washington, DC

Cover Photographs: Left: Debbie Henry, Center: Andrea Foster, Right: Ralph Newell

Illustrations: Max-Karl Winkler

The following photographs from the Nikon 1997 International Small World Competition Winners are reproduced in this book

Nikon #1. First Place, **Babara Danowski** (page 65); Nikon #2. Second Place, **Stephen Rogers** (page 71); Nikon #3. Third Place, **K. G. Murti** (page 77); Nikon #4. Fourth Place, **David K. Terbush** (page 69); Nikon #5. Fifth Place, **Marc Van Hove** (page 57); Nikon #7. Seventh Place, **Dennis Kunkel** (page 68); Nikon #9. Ninth Place, **Ulrich Büttner** (page 49); Nikon #12. Twelfth Place, **Heiti Paves** (page 71); Nikon #13. Thirteenth Place, **Sükrü Yilmaz** (page 107); Nikon #14. Fourteenth Place, **M. I. Walker** (page 124); Nikon #15. Fifteenth Place, **Kevin A. Edwards** (page 67); Nikon #17 Seventeenth Place, **Karl E. Deckart** (page 27); Nikon #20. Twentieth Place, **Norman Barker**, RPB (page 93)

Honorable Mentions: Nikon #HM1, **K. Gardner** (page 87); Nikon #HM2, **Mark Gesell** (page 37); Nikon #HM3, **Margaret Oechsli** (page 115); Nikon #HM4, **Jonathan Witt** (page 75)

Nikon International Small World Competition recognizes leading scientists, researchers, and others from around the world for their unique and valuable work in photography through the microscope. Images from this outstanding collection of photographs embody an intrinsic aesthetic beauty that represents an art form unique to this competition. NSTA sincerely thanks Nikon for permission to use these award-winning photomicrographs. For further information, phone (516) 547-8569.

Stock Number: PB 125X
ISBN Number: 0-87355-166-4

Table Of Contents

Introduction

ANDREA FOSTER

I t is rare for a profession to reach national consensus about its vision for change. The National Science Education Standards represent just such a landmark effort. Science educators, scientists, administrators, businesspeople, and concerned citizens, with very different perspectives have joined forces to speak eloquently for science education in our schools.

The very breadth of the Standards may seem intimidating at first—something for everyone—but nothing for tomorrow's lesson. So, for middle level teachers across America, we offer this practical guidebook, *NSTA Pathways to the Science Standards: Guidelines for Moving the Vision into Practice.*

In these pages, we demonstrate how you can carry the vision of the Standards—for teaching, professional development, assessment, content, program, and system—into the real world of your classroom and school. This book is also a tool for you to use in collaborating with principals, local and state administrators, parents, school board members, and other stakeholders in science education.

Pathways was created by an impressive partnership of teachers and administrators who believe that many elements of the Standards are already in place today. Great science education happens in many middle level classrooms, and today's teachers *can* achieve the teaching and learning detailed in these Standards now and in the coming decades.

Many Options, No One Way

In middle level schools nationwide, the Standards and the *NSTA Pathways to the Science Standards* will spark changes that will spring from the strengths of each school faculty and the unique character of each community. Because there is no one correct pathway to achieve the goals of the Standards, this *Pathways* book presents a variety of ways, through suggestions and models, to help middle level teachers begin to implement the Standards.

You can start by building on what works well today in your classroom and school. Several types of pilot projects and established programs that illustrate the vision of excellence can be found in many classrooms across the country. Depending on resources, commitment, and interests, each middle level teacher, each school, and each community will follow a different pathway in reaching for the vision of the Standards.

Basic Principles in the Standards

All students can learn science, and all students should have the opportunity to become scientifically literate. This is one of the strongest of the four fundamental themes of the National Science Education

Standards. This effort, begun in the early grades when students are naturally curious about the world around them, must be expanded at the middle level when students are interested in investigating relationships, applying science to their daily lives, considering implications for society and the environment, and beginning to make personal career decisions. The essential experiences of science inquiry, exploration, and application must be provided to *every* student in the nation from kindergarten through grade 12.

Another strong theme in the Standards is that *learning science is an active process.* The Standards rest solidly on the foundation of education research which demonstrates that learning is an active process achieved by enthusiastic and motivated students. Much of the literature that supports this perspective presents the notion of "constructivism" to emphasize the student's role in building and understanding concepts.

A third theme, *school science reflects the intellectual and cultural traditions that characterize the practice of contemporary science* speaks to the importance of providing students with authentic sci-

ence experiences. The isolated laboratory exercises, designed to validate knowledge already obtained are giving way to involving students in the analysis of critical community, national, and global issues.

The fourth key principle, *improving science education is part of systemic education reform,* acknowledges the role of the teacher in making the Standards a reality, but states, in no uncertain terms, that the burden cannot be placed upon teachers alone. For real reform to occur, all levels and all stakeholders must come to a common vision.

Beginning the Journey

The primary strength of the National Science Education Standards is the process through which its vision was created: a consensus of divergent viewpoints forged of shared commitment. The document paints a clear picture of what should be taught (content standards), how to do it (teaching and program standards), how you will know when you get there (assessment standards), and how to build capacity for change (professional development and education system standards).

We invite you to use this book to design your own pathway for capturing the vision of the National Science Education Standards and making it real in your classroom and school.

How To Use This Book

This *NSTA Pathways to the Science Standards* has one audience—you, the middle level teacher. As your guide to the National Science Education Standards, *Pathways* provides practical ideas for capturing the vision of the Standards and making it real in your classroom.

The first three and last two chapters of the book discuss the Standards that apply to teachers of all grade levels: Teaching, Professional Development, Assessment, Program, and System Standards. Many of the recommended pathways are the same regardless of the level that you teach. For this reason, there will be many similarities in these sections of the three companion *Pathways*. In each of these chapters you will

find a discussion of the Standards followed by Resources for the Road—a list of pertinent articles, most of them from *Science and Children*, *Science Scope*, and *The Science Teacher*. You will be able to access the NSTA-published articles on the CD that supplements this book. Each of the five K–12 Standards ends with a Changing Emphases chart.

It is important to remember that efforts toward change and improvement in each of the five Standards areas mentioned above must occur if the students are to achieve the Content Standards. As the Standards point out, middle level teachers are not expected to be the *sole* agents of change. The effort requires the support of principals, local and state

administrators, parents, legislators, volunteers, business representatives, and interested citizens working together.

The fourth chapter of *Pathways* reviews the nature of the learner at middle level and examines the science goals for middle level students as outlined in the eight sections of the Content Standards. Each of the Content sections begins with a comparison of that Standard at the three levels followed by "Building Conceptual Bridges." These are followed by an exploratory view of "A Classroom in Action" with notations in the margin that provide vista points for reflecting on effective teaching and assessment strategies. The specific content standards show how to build conceptual

RALPH NEWELL

NASA

bridges between the Elementary Standards and High School Standards. The remaining parts of the Content sections address practical ways to develop an understanding of concepts, challenges, misconceptions, and connections to other fields of science. Resources for the Road augment the chapter.

The book has four appendices, including a history of the Science Standards movement, a complete list of all the National Science Education Standards, recommendations for setting up a middle level science facility, and a list of addresses for middle level science programs.

Pathways is for using and sharing. It will enable you to identify, create, and implement classroom experiences that will have power and value for your students and improve science learning in your classroom.

Pathways has key information that you can share with those who determine policy and make decisions at district and state levels. You can be an agent of change. Share this book with principals, local and state administrators, your board of education, policymakers, parents, business representatives, and other citizens to help them understand what is needed in your classroom to prepare your students for the 21st century.

Enjoy using *Pathways*. As you travel along, remember there are many routes you can take to reach for the vision of the National Science Education Standards. Enjoy the journey!

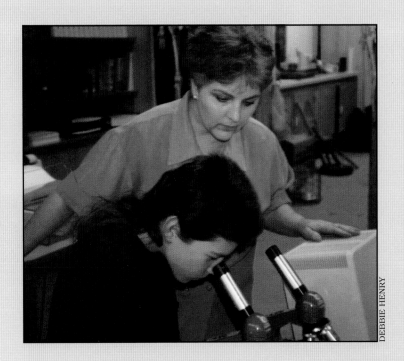

DEBBIE HENRY

Science
Teaching
Standards

As teachers, we are the most important force in the education system. We are the key to reform.

Realizing the Teaching Standards

As teachers, you are the most important component in the education system. You are the individuals who will chart the way to implement the National Science Education Standards in your classroom and school. How your students learn science depends on you. To assist you, the Standards suggest new ways to approach the teaching and learning of science.

First, they urge teachers to recognize that science is a discipline that must be taught to *every* student in *every* middle level school and that it must be taught using an inquiry/ thinking approach. Science has an important place in the school curriculum.

The Standards reassure teachers that they, like their students, are lifelong learners. The Standards offer ideas for becoming more professional whether you currently teach science with confidence or with a feeling of discomfort.

Becoming an Expert

The Standards urge teachers to set higher personal standards for their instruction and to become proficient at:

TIE BUDZINSKY

- facilitating ideas as students investigate as individuals or in collaborative groups
- budgeting time, allowing inquiries to be explored and not cut off by a ringing bell
- assessing progress by observing students, asking effective questions, and evaluating written work (both formally and informally), thereby determining what changes need to occur to improve instruction and learning
- allowing students to inquire, explore, and experiment in depth, over days and perhaps weeks
- providing and maintaining materials and equipment for students to use in collaborating with colleagues

- integrating across science disciplines and integrating science with other subject areas.

(For the complete text of the National Science Education Standards, see Appendix B.)

Both the Teaching Standards and the Content Standards put high value on "inquiry" as an important component of science teaching and learning. Inquiry is a natural process in which individuals ask questions, gather information through many and varied activities, examine data, and develop explanations about the data to answer the original question. Inquiry is basic to science itself—it is how scientists work. Giving students opportunities to inquire is a vital component in helping them become scientifically literate.

Although all students have the capacity to inquire, that capacity changes and becomes more sophisticated as students mature and gain experience. Younger adolescents explore questions with trial-and-error experiences and experiments, and they are introduced to testing by learning about variables and establishing controls. As adolescents develop cognitively, they become capable of using more formal thinking skills, such as the manipulation of several variables and using abstract thinking. It is important, then, that teachers become expert at facilitating quality inquiry experiences appropriate for the students they teach. To do this, teachers must use their knowledge of adolescent development and their familiarity with the learning characteristics and styles of their students. Teachers must provide the appropriate classroom setting for students to carry out inquiry investigations if the best possible science learning is to occur.

Constructing Their Own Knowledge

Ideas for improving the teaching and learning of science grew from a body of research that supports the National Science Education Standards and the current science education reform movement.

We now know that students don't learn simply by listening to someone talk or by reading a book. In other words, we cannot just transfer, or hand over our own understanding of the natural world to young adolescents. We cannot just show and tell. As the Standards point out, students have to construct, or build, their *own* knowledge in "a process that is individual and social." Students have to take an active role in their own learning. This teaching/learning relationship is called constructivism.

Research strongly supports the idea that middle level students learn best by building their own knowledge through appropriate concrete experiences. Because students acquire knowledge at different paces and through different learning styles, teachers need to provide instruction that is flexible and sensitive to these differences.

It is important that teachers choose what they want their students to learn with thoughtfulness. They should engage students in ideas that are relevant to the learner and likely to serve the student well over a lifetime. It is also important to recognize that not all hands-on experiences are constructive experiences. Recipe-type experiences, in which students follow directions to replicate an experiment or build a model, are not constructive experiences. One-time activities are also not constructive experiences.

Helping Students Learn

The role of teachers is to help students construct accurate concepts, use process skills, develop positive scientific attitudes, and recognize incorrect ideas. Teachers engage students, structure time, create a setting, make tools available, identify resources, assess students' progress, and guide students' self-assessment.

Here is how you can apply the constructivist approach:
• *Begin by assessing student preconceptions.* Until you

know what preconceptions and knowledge students have about a topic, building new ideas will be difficult. Interviews, questions, drawings, predictions, and group discussions help uncover preconceptions.

- *Build on past experience.* Meaning is created in a student's mind when concrete, physical experiences interact with existing beliefs. When an experience contradicts prior knowledge, the child may become surprised, frustrated—and more eager to learn.
- *Start with concrete experiences.* Provide students with hands-on experiences that help them to develop their own understanding and vocabulary. Use these hands-on experiences as a bridge to introduce the vocabulary and concepts of science.
- *Take sufficient time.* Acquiring new knowledge can only happen if a student is given unhurried experiences and the motivation to allow learning to happen.
- *Foster continuing inquiry.* Through questioning, self-assessment, and open-ended investigations, constructivist teachers provide environments that challenge students to learn.
- *Encourage students to reflect on their own thinking.* When students question their own thinking, they develop higher levels of critical thinking skills and attitudes of a life-long learner.

Asking Questions

Good questions excite and motivate students. Good questions are open-ended—they don't have one right answer. Open-ended questions might ask, "What if?"; "What do you think will happen next?"; "What do you think we should do?"; and "Can you tell me more about that?" Teachers asking open-ended questions avoid questions that have only "yes" or "no" answers and questions that rely on quick memory recall.

When students are asked open-ended questions, they will pose innovative questions of their own, thus expanding their own capacity for creative thinking and problem-solving. Teachers learn about students through the answers they give, but even more from the questions they ask.

Learning to ask, pace, and interpret good questions are vital skills in classrooms where the Standards guide science learning. Good questions support inquiry, provide ongoing assessment of student progress, and can be used to guide the pace of instruction.

Science for All

Young adolescents differ in many ways, and teachers must adjust their instruction to meet the different needs of students. In your classroom there will inevitably be students with various learning styles; from different racial, ethnic, and cultural backgrounds; and with a variety of special needs.

How can teachers support diverse learners in their classrooms while working to build a real community of learners? First, by modeling acceptance and tolerance. Second, by consciously choosing methods and assessments that support individual learning styles. And, third, by recognizing that much learning occurs during the interactions of students with one another and with the teacher.

Six Teaching Standards

In addition to promoting the use of inquiry and the constructivist approach in science teaching, the Standards address other teaching-related issues relevant to effective practice. The Standards envision middle level teachers becoming more expert at:
• selecting or planning an inquiry-based science program for their students
• guiding and facilitating science learning
• engaging in ongoing assessment of his or her teaching and of student learning
• designing and managing learning environments that provide students with the time, space, and resources needed for learning science
• developing communities of science learners that reflect the intellectual rigor of sci-

entific inquiry and the social values conducive to science learning
• participating actively in the ongoing planning and development of their school science program.

For a list of all the National Science Education Standards, see Appendix B.

Filling in the Gaps

To carry out the goals of these Standards, teachers themselves must continue to be students of human learning,

science subject matter, and pedagogy. Expert teachers are knowledgeable in all three domains.

A teacher need not be a professional scientist to be a quality teacher of middle level science, but he or she needs to be scientifically literate and have the interest to continue learning more and more science. The Science Standards stress that quality teaching involves knowledge in each discipline as well as skill at blending that knowledge through effective teaching strategies.

JUANITA J. MATKINS

Abdi, S. Wali. (1995, September). Middle School Students: What a Teacher Needs to Know. *Science Scope, 19* (1), 37–39.

Adkins, Carol. (1996, April). Ten Steps to Better Simulations. *Science Scope, 19* (7), 28–29.

Andersen, Hans O. (1991, May). Y'all Can. *Science Scope, 14* (8), 28–31.

Armstrong, Thomas. (1994). *Multiple Intelligences in the Classroom.* Alexandria, VA: Association for Supervision and Curriculum Development (ASCD).

Atwater, Mary M. (1995, October). The Cross-Curricular Classroom. *Science Scope, 19* (2), 42–45.

Bellamy, Nedaro. (1994, March). Bias in the Classroom: Are We Guilty? *Science Scope, 17* (6), 60–63.

Blosser, Patricia E. (1991). *How To Ask the Right Questions.* Arlington, VA: National Science Teachers Association (NSTA).

Carey, Shelley Johnson (Ed.). (1993). *Science for All Cultures.* Arlington, VA: National Science Teachers Association (NSTA).

Chahrour, Janet. (1994, October). Perfecting the Question. *Science Scope, 18* (2), 9–11.

Hampton, Elaine, and **Gallegos, Charles**. (1994, March). Science for All Students. *Science Scope, 17* (6), 5–6, 7.

Hewitt, Patricia, Odell, Michael R. L., and Worch, Eric A. (1995, November/December). Models Make It Better. *Science Scope, 19* (3), 26–29.

Huber, Richard A., and **Walker, Bradford L.** (1996, September). Science Reading Dos and Don'ts. *Science Scope, 20* (1) 22–23.

Ivy, Tamra. (1994, March). Turning an Educator's Vision into a Classroom Reality. *Science Scope, 17* (6), 10–14.

Keys, Carolyn W. (1996, February). Inquiring Minds Want To Know. *Science Scope, 19* (5), 17–19.

Leach, Lisa S. (1994, March). Sexism in the Classroom: A Self-Quiz for Teachers. *Science Scope, 17* (6), 54–59.

Liftig, Inez. (1995, November/December). Crystal-Clear Teaching. *Science Scope, 19* (3), 14–18.

Liggitt-Fox, Dianna. (1997, February). Fighting Student Misconceptions: Three Effective Strategies. *Science Scope, 20* (5), 28–30.

Ossont, Dave. (1993, May). How I Use Cooperative Learning. *Science Scope, 16* (8) 28–31.

Roth, Wolff-Michael, and **Bowen, Michael.** (1993, January). Maps for More Meaningful Learning. *Science Scope, 16* (4), 24–25.

Schulte, Paige L. (1996, November/December). A Definition of Constructivism. *Science Scope, 20* (3), 25–27.

Simons, Grace H., and **Hepner, Nancy.** (1992, September). The Special Student in Science. *Science Scope, 16* (1), 34–39, 54.

Stepans, Joseph, and **Veath, M. Lois.** (1994, May). How Do Students Really Explain Changes in Matter? *Science Scope, 17* (8), 31–35.

Sumrall, William J. (1997, January). Why Avoid Hands-on Science? *Science Scope, 20* (4), 16–19.

Young Jay A. (1997, March). Chemical Safety. *Science Scope, 64* (3), 43–45.

Young Jay A. (1997, April). Chemical Safety. *Science Scope, 64* (4), 40–41.

Changing Emphases

The National Science Education Standards envision change throughout the system. The Teaching Standards encompass the following changes in emphases:

LESS EMPHASIS ON	MORE EMPHASIS ON
Treating all students alike and responding to the group as a whole	Understanding and responding to individual student's interests, strengths, experiences, and needs
Rigidly following curriculum	Selecting and adapting curriculum
Focusing on student acquisition of information	Focusing on student understanding and use of scientific knowledge, ideas, and inquiry processes
Presenting scientific knowledge through lecture, text, and demonstration	Guiding students in active and extended scientific inquiry
Asking for recitation of acquired knowledge	Providing opportunities for scientific discussion and debate among students
Testing students for factual information at the end of the unit or chapter	Continuously assessing student understanding
Maintaining responsibility and authority	Sharing responsibility for learning with students
Supporting competition	Supporting a classroom community with cooperation, shared responsibility, and respect
Working alone	Working with other teachers to enhance the science program

Reprinted with permission from the *National Science Education Standards*. © 1996 National Academy of Sciences. Courtesy of the National Academy Press, Washington, D.C.

RUTH RUUD

Professional Development Standards

The Standards challenge us to become dedicated, lifelong learners.

Reaching for the Professional Development Standards

MICHELE B. BIFELT

Professional development is a career-long endeavor. No matter the field (medicine, law, teaching), a degree does not make one an excellent practitioner. Experience certainly helps, but continual learning must be a major career commitment for all professionals, including teachers of every grade level.

The Standards urge elementary teachers to become lifelong learners so that they can expand their knowledge of science content and learning theories, thus becoming more skilled at pedagogy and inquiry.

According to the Standards, professional development for teachers of science requires:
- learning essential science content through the perspectives and methods of inquiry
- integrating knowledge of science, learning, pedagogy, and students, and applying that knowledge to science learning

- building the understanding and the ability for lifelong learning
- professional development programs that are coherent and integrated.

Setting Personal Goals

The Professional Development Standards (for the full text, see Appendix B) challenge each teacher to set personal goals for professional development. The Standards put the responsibility for achieving these goals squarely on the shoulders of teachers. Professional development is not the responsibility of administrators, school boards, or school systems and districts, although these groups *must* make significant contributions to science education, including supporting teachers' efforts in professional development.

For many teachers who have grown to expect their district to provide the professional development program, the Standards set new expectations. (It may also set higher expectations for school administrators who may be encouraged to try new inservice programs.)

The Professional Development Standards relate to what teachers need to know about science and learning and how they effectively transfer that knowledge to teaching. Clearly the intent of these Standards cannot be accomplished in a one-day inservice workshop. The learning will span an entire career.

Understanding Science

The first two Professional Development Standards describe the essential content and elements of teaching. Adequate content is described as a "broad base of understanding" in both science disciplines and learning theory.

Middle level teachers should have a broad understanding of science content but are also expected to be familiar with at least one science discipline. Middle level teachers also need an understanding of mathematics and technology, especially as these disciplines relate to sci-

ence. All middle level teachers need to know how to use the process of inquiry, how content knowledge is attained, and how to use science process skills. The essence of science is not the content alone, but the process of inquiry through which the content was derived.

Another way to say it is that knowledge is not simply what we know, but how we come to know it. For example, it may be interesting to know the distance to a planet or star (a content fact), but it is even more interesting and appropriate from a science viewpoint to know how the human mind measures that distance without being able to traverse it.

NANCY ROEHM

Understanding Learning

The Standards support the growing body of research about learning theory. Because we now know that learning is not passive, teachers need to develop expertise and not merely convey knowledge verbally.

Teachers need to know how young adolescents learn—cognitively, socially, and psychologically—so that they can adjust their instruction to meet the different developmental capabilities and learning styles of their students.

This knowledge is critical for making decisions about what to teach, how to pace instruction, and how to select, adapt, or create appropriate curriculum and instructional activities wisely.

Teachers also need to develop expertise in knowing the difference between effective hands-on activities and ineffective science hands-on activities. They need proficiency in asking questions, guiding discussions, and organizing students into cooperative and collaborative groupings. They need skill in assessing what students know and what they can do.

What's New?

Professional development programs in the 1990s look different from the programs teachers have known in the past. According to Sparks (1995), today's programs are focused on schools, not districts, and concentrate on student needs (not adult needs). Professional activities let teachers themselves study rather than turning tasks over to "visiting experts." Staff developers serve as facilitators, not trainers. Staff development is seen as indispensable, as in every profession, and thus no longer considered a frill.

Choose Your Pathway

There are many pathways for you to take as you work toward achieving the Professional Development Standards. Here are a few of them:

Graduate Courses

One of the most common ways to improve knowledge is enrolling in graduate courses. Some of these courses provide opportunities for additional learning in the laboratory, in research, and in teaching skills. They often discuss why some strategies work well in classrooms. Many colleges and universities give teachers the opportunity to design individual programs around a set of courses to work toward an advanced degree.

Structured Inservice Programs

Today, many school systems allow staff committees to design departmental, building, or district inservice programs. Some local resources, such as science centers, museums, and industries, plan programs specifically for classroom teachers. Teachers attending these programs in teams, accompanied by a school administrator, become more effective in transferring what they have learned to the school setting. The most effective staff development programs are long-range (not one-shot workshops) that model the information.

Professional Associations

Thousands of teachers attend national and regional conferences sponsored by professional associations. NSTA sponsors one national and three regional conventions on science education/teaching each year. For the cost of registration, teachers can select from hundreds of workshops. In addition, the exhibits are expansive, and there are numerous opportunities to network with other teachers.

Journals

Membership in a professional association makes available professional journals (such as *Science & Children*, *Science Scope* and *The Science Teacher* from NSTA), newspapers, and newsletters that bring classroom science ideas and news to your doorstep.

Collaboration with Other Professionals

Teaching is no longer a private endeavor. Collaboration and team teaching are enriching instruction. Non-threatening coaching by a fellow teacher of science can offer additional opportunities for discovering other styles, strategies, and options for teaching science. Mentoring (whether formal or informal) is another form of collaboration for giving and receiving feedback about the teaching and learning that occurs in classrooms.

Self-Reflection and Inquiry

Not all learning experiences need to involve structured meetings, nor do they need to be group-oriented. There is much value in reading, studying, and exploring on your own. In fact, an important component of any career-long professional development plan must be self-reflective inquiry. As we try new ideas, we might use journals, audiotapes, and videotapes to track our progress.

Evaluation

Using evaluation as a vehicle for professional development will seem strange to most teachers. New, more reflective systems for evaluation, such as teacher portfolios, can become valuable opportunities for teachers to talk with other educators about classroom decisions involving curriculum, delivery, and climate. If evaluation is to be a tool for growth, however, teachers must be full partners in developing the evaluation system.

School Improvement for Professional Growth

Setting common goals can provide a school- or district-wide impetus for professional development. A shared direction (such as redesigning the science program) can prompt a group to determine what strategy or plan has the best hope of success. Most plans include regular evaluation of progress. Having a voice in the policies and procedures that affect their classrooms will certainly increase teachers' sense of ownership and dedication.

Other Possibilities

Internships in industry or research establishments provide new perspectives for science teachers. Travel (either to scientific sites or to other classrooms) has long been considered one of the most motivating professional development resources.

Closer to home, exploration of the World Wide Web, including the NSTA Web site at http://www.nsta.org/ or online networks, can yield a wealth of resources and the opportunity to find answers to questions and share ideas with colleagues.

The possibilities for professional development are limitless. The critical question is "How does this experience move me toward my personal goal of becoming the best teacher I can be?"

Howe, Ann C., and **Stubbs, Harriett S.** (1997, August). Empowering Science Teachers: A Model for Professional Development. *Journal of Science Teacher Education, 8* (3), 167–182.

Mason, Cheryl. (1993). *Preparing and Directing a Teacher Institute.* Arlington, VA: National Science Teachers Association (NSTA).

National Science Teachers Association (NSTA). (1992). *NSTA Standards for Science Teacher Preparation.* Arlington, VA: Author. Adopted by the National Council for Accreditation of Teacher Education (NCATE).

Nichols, Sharon E., Tippins, Deborah, and **Wiseman, Katherine.** (1997, May). A Toolkit for Developing Critically Reflective Science Teachers. *Journal of Science Teacher Education, 8* (2), 77–106.

Parke, Helen M., and **Coble, Charles R.** (1997, October). Teachers Designing Curriculum as Professional Development: A Model for Transformational Science Teaching. *Journal of Research in Science Teaching, 34* (8), 773–789.

Sparks, Dennis. (1995, Winter). A Paradigm Shift in Staff Development. In Professional Development. (Theme Issue). *ERIC Review, 3* (3), 2-4. Available at http://www.aspensys.com/eric/ter/.

Changing Emphases

The National Science Education Standards envision change throughout the system. The Professional Development Standards encompass the following changes in emphases:

LESS EMPHASIS ON	MORE EMPHASIS ON
Transmission of teaching knowledge and skills by lectures	Inquiry into teaching and learning
Learning science by lecture and reading	Learning science through investigation and inquiry
Separation of science and teaching knowledge	Integration of science and teaching knowledge
Separation of theory and practice	Integration of theory and practice in school settings
Individual learning	Collegial and collaborative learning
Fragmented, one-shot sessions	Long-term coherent plans
Courses and workshops	A variety of professional development activities
Reliance on external expertise	Mix of internal and external expertise
Staff developers as educators	Staff developers as facilitators, consultants, and planners
Teacher as technician	Teacher as intellectual, reflective practitioner
Teacher as consumer of knowledge about teaching	Teacher as producer of knowledge about teaching
Teacher as follower	Teacher as leader
Teacher as an individual based in a classroom	Teacher as member of a collegial professional community
Teacher as target of change	Teacher as source and facilitator of change

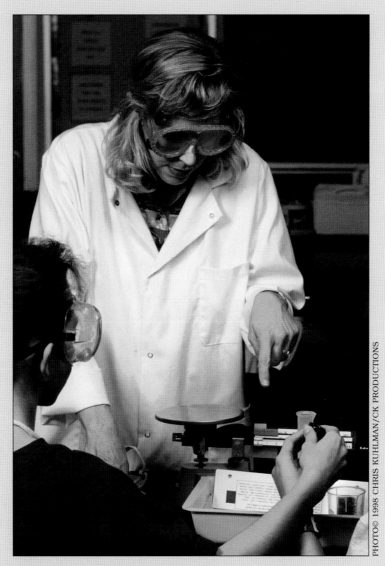

Assessment Standards

Assessment does not only occur during test time, it is a continuing, dynamic process.

Exploring the Assessment Standards

Assessment is an ongoing process, essential for establishing and maintaining an effective instructional program in science. Assessment involves gathering information to answer such questions as: What are the present levels of student understanding? What have students achieved? How much progress has been made toward the learning goals? Have the expectations suggested by the Standards been met? Which lessons or units are successful? Which programs are successful? What changes need to be made? Assessment contributes to policy making, funding, evaluating curricular decisions, certification standards, and educational theory.

Assessing Students

The five Assessment Standards for science at the middle level address the following:

- assessments are carried out for specific purposes, therefore the data and the methods used to collect the data should address those purposes. Teachers need to know the strengths and limitations of the assessment strategies that they choose, and be able to explain them to those who are affected.

- assessing achievement should focus on the content that has the greatest importance to learning. This includes knowing how to conduct inquiries, reason scientifically, use science when making personal and social decisions, communicate effectively, and understand science concepts and principles.

- assessment measures achievement and takes a careful look at the opportunities that students have for learning. Student preparation, access to experience, and the condition of the learning environment, contribute to the context in which students are assessed and affect assess-

ment outcomes.

- Data support and drive decisions about students, teachers, programs, and systems. There must be confidence in the technical quality of the data, and for this reason, assessments must be valid, authentic, and reliable. Results of different assessment strategies must be consistent. The degree of confidence that decision-makers place in the data must be consistent with the consequences of the decisions to be made.

- in assessment, as in teaching, care must always be taken to avoid stereotyping and being biased. Learners have different styles and their perspectives vary,

based on their backgrounds, the environment, or areas of ability.

- assessment practices must accommodate diversity, and assessment data must be examined for signs of bias. The use of statistics for data from large populations is valuable when interpreting results.
- assessment data influence how we think about instruction, science programs and student progress. It is important to identify the assumptions applied to the data and to describe the context within which an assessment is carried out.
- the guidelines provided by the Assessment Standards suggest a range of ways for carrying out assessment, including non-traditional methods; projects that take hours or days to complete; tasks that involve students applying science knowledge; and portfolios that include products representing student accomplishment. When teachers implement well-designed science curricula that engage students in inquiry, scientific thinking, and problem-solving, they find traditional assessment practices limiting and inadequate for determining what students understand and can do. As curricula, programs, and teachers change, the methods and targets of assessment will also change.

Sharing the Message

Teachers can gain support for their own changes in practice by sharing the straightforward messages of the Assessment Standards.

Good teachers assess their students continually. Assessment does not only occur during test time, it is a continuing, dynamic process. Assessment and instruction complement each other, interweaving through the entire science program.

Assessments gauge the opportunities that students have for learning, and their ability to take advantage of these opportunities. Comparisons of test results between districts and states may reveal differences in facilities, resources, and other support systems that affect the opportunities for learning.

A balance of assessment strategies allows teachers to form a well-rounded picture of student learning in science at the middle level, and provides a diversity of opportunity for students to demonstrate success.

Assessments must be fair and unbiased and, like teaching, they must accommodate the differences of individual students.

New types of assessment may take time and may look very different from the ones with which students and parents are familiar. Explaining assessment purposes, processes, and results to students, educators, parents, and community members, contributes to a good relationship between the school and the community, and to informed decision-making beyond the classroom.

Using Multiple Strategies

Assessment provides a means for teachers to measure the learning achieved by each individual student as well as by the whole class. Traditional paper-and-pencil tests and evaluations of products, such as reports and displays, provide data that can be recorded easily for use in progress reports and grading. Teachers often know from other kinds of observations that certain students "got it." The challenge, then, is to record student success by gathering

PHOTO© 1998 CHRIS KUHLMAN/CK PRODUCTIONS

PHOTO© 1998 CHRIS KUHLMAN/CK PRODUCTIONS

evidence in a variety of ways and using information from many sources to decide on levels of achievement, effectiveness of a program, and on plans for change.

Students who learn in different ways and excel through natural ability are served best by teachers who use diverse instructional strategies. It follows, then, that students should be assessed using different approaches so that every student is given a fair chance to demonstrate science learning. At the middle level, there are many opportunities for gathering information about what students know in science and how they are thinking. Each type of assessment has its strengths and limitations. The examples described here suggest a range of possibilities:

Traditional paper and pencil, short answer, multiple choice, true or false, and *fill-in-the-blank tests.* These require the ability to read, and they test specific knowledge. Although higher level thinking may be involved, students are typically engaged in recall or recognition. The advantages of these methods are that evaluation is rapid, producing numerical scores, and large groups can be tested at the same time.

Traditional short essay test. Students need to be able to read, listen, and write in order to take these tests. Although higher level thinking can be involved, and specific knowledge can be verified, typically, students are engaged in organizing recalled information. This type of test is evaluated using a match to expected responses, or a rubric. Useful qualitative and quantitative records are produced.

Pictorial-based testing, involving interaction with photographs, movies, diagrams, and other visual media, including drawings by the student. This form of assessment can be particularly useful for students with limited English proficiency.

Written reports, video or multimedia presentation, displays, models, illustrations, and other archival evidence of individual or group effort are used in these tests. Students are able to demonstrate expertise and knowledge, pictorially, and spatially, as well as in the traditional verbal, logical, and mathematical modes. These tests address students' special interests, thematic units or topics, and interdisciplinary approaches to instruction and assessment.

Performance based assessment. One or more students complete a task using a variety of observable skills, demonstrating knowledge within a meaningful or authentic context. The teacher is able to see the results of student effort and the process used to find answers. The tasks model the kind of activities that usually take place during science instruction.

Portfolios are collections of examples of student work gathered over time, even over years, ideally involving student input in determining the contents. Individual talent and progress can be demonstrated. The time committed to this assessment process often overlaps student consultation time. Storage problems can be alleviated by adopting electronic formats.

Science journals capture a dimension of students' conceptual understanding that is different from that which is usually measured by other means. Students can record procedures and results from investigations as well as observations, hypotheses, and inferences about science phenomena. Journals include student-rendered scientific illustrations, diagrams, and other pictorial devices for communicating complex ideas. Teachers assess students' ability to organize information and to communicate independent thinking over a period of time.

Group projects offer special opportunities as well as challenges for noting student contributions to collaborative efforts.

Anecdotal information recorded by the teacher provides additional assessment information and often produces or confirms insights not evident by other means. Anecdotes are considered along with other kinds of data and have particular value for individualizing the assessment process and capturing elements of students' learning that cannot easily be quantified.

Standardized tests allow students to be assessed or evaluated and compared to a large population. Results are valuable tools for developing programs and confirming their effectiveness. Like all tests or assessments, standardized tests have their strengths and limitations.

Assessment in the Service of Change

Perhaps the greatest gains for middle level teachers in including challenging and interesting alternative strategies for assessment are the expanded control over self-reflection on teaching effectiveness and in increasing the control students have over monitoring their own progress. Teachers are encouraged to use a variety of assessment strategies for studying and effecting change in instructional practice, observing learner characteristics, and providing fair opportunities for each student to demonstrate success.

Changing Emphases

The National Science Education Standards envision change throughout the system. The Assessment Standards encompass the following changes in emphases:

LESS EMPHASIS ON	MORE EMPHASIS ON
Assessing what is easily measured	Assessing what is most highly valued
Assessing discrete knowledge	Assessing rich, well-structured knowledge
Assessing scientific knowledge	Assessing scientific understanding and reasoning
Assessing to learn what students do not know	Assessing to learn what students do understand
Assessing only achievement	Assessing achievement and opportunity to learn
End-of-term assessment by teachers	Students engaged in ongoing assessment of their work and that of others
Development of external assessments by measurement experts alone	Teachers involved in the development of external assessments

Reprinted with permission from the *National Science Education Standards.* © 1996 National Academy of Sciences. Courtesy of the National Academy Press, Washington, D.C.

RESOURCES FOR THE ROAD

Association for Supervision and Curriculum Development (ASCD). (1995). *Designing Performance Assessment Tasks*. Arlington, VA: Author.

Bonnstetter, Ronald J. (1992, March). Where Can Teachers Go for More Information on Portfolios? *Science Scope, 15* (6), 28.

Collins, Angelo. (1992, March.) Portfolios: Questions for Design. *Science Scope, 15* (6), 25–27.

Doran, Rodney L., and **Hejaily, Nicholas.** (1992, March). Hands-on Evaluation: A How-To Guide. *Science Scope, 15* (6), 9–11.

Doran, Rodney L., Lawrenz, Frances, and **Helgeson, Stanley.** (1994). Research on Assessment in Science, in Gabel, Dorothy L. (Ed.), *Handbook of Research on Science Teaching and Learning,* New York: Macmillan Publishing, 388–442.

Finson, Kevin D., and **Beaver, John B.** (1994, September). Performance Assessment: Getting Started. *Science Scope, 18* (1), 44–49.

Freedman, Robin Lee Harris. (1994). *Open-ended Questioning.* Menlo Park, CA: Addison-Wesley.

Gondree, Lillian L., and **Tundo, Valerie.** (1996, April). An Alternative Final Evaluation. *Science Scope, 19* (7), 18–21.

Hart, Diane. (1994). *Authentic Assessment: A Handbook for Educators.* Menlo Park, CA: Addison-Wesley.

Hein, George E. (Ed.). (1990). *The Assessment of Hands-On Elementary Science Programs.* Fargo, ND: Center for Teaching and Learning, University of North Dakota.

Hein, George E., and **Price, Sabra.** (1994). *Active Assessment for Science: A Guide for Elementary School Teachers.* Portsmouth, NJ: Heinemann.

Herman, Joan L., Aschbacher, Pamela R., and **Winters, Lynn.** (1992). *A Practical Guide to Alternative Assessment.* Alexandria, VA: Association for Supervision and Curriculum Development (ASCD).

Liftig, Inez Fugate, Liftig, Bob, and **Eaker, Karen.** (1992, March). Making Assessment Work: What Teachers Should Know Before They Try It. *Science Scope, 15* (6), 4, 6, 8.

Logan, Jerry. (1996, March). Authoring Your Own Digital Portfolio Assessment. *Science Scope, 19* (6), 48–49.

Luft, Julie. (1997, February). Design Your Own Rubric. *Science Scope, 20* (5), 25–27.

Moran, Jeffrey B., and **Boulter, William.** (1992, March). Step-by-Step Scoring. *Science Scope, 15* (6), 46–47, 59.

Nott, Linda, Reeve, Colleen, and **Reeve, Raymond.** (1992, March). Scoring Rubrics: An Assessment Option. *Science Scope, 15* (6), 44–45.

O'Neil, J. Peter. (1994, January). Portfolio Pointers. *Science Scope, 17* (4), 32.

Roth, Wolff-Michael. (1992, March). Dynamic Evaluation. *Science Scope, 15* (6), 37–40.

Smith, Paul G. (1995, September). Reveling in Rubrics. *Science Scope, 19* (1), 34–36.

Tippins, Deborah J., and **Dana, Nancy Fichtman.** (1992, March). Culturally Relevant Alternative Assessment. *Science Scope, 15* (6), 50–53.

Content Standards

All parts of the education system must work together and, in the process, support us in moving toward the vision of the Standards.

Mapping the Content Standards

The Content Standards offer us much more than just a traditional listing of content objectives. The Standards recognize that middle level students are going through tremendous changes and that effective teaching must address these changes if learning is to be meaningful. The Standards shift the emphasis from presenting scientific knowledge through lecture and demonstration to encouraging active learning in which students learn with understanding.

The Standards emphasize that, for middle level students, the essence of learning science lies not in memorizing facts, but in carrying out the processes of inquiry by ask-ing questions, making obser-vations, and gathering, orga-nizing, and analyzing data. It is through these inquiries that students develop life-long thinking skills.

But content is not ne-glected. The emphasis has shifted from rote memorization of taxonomies and tables to an understanding of the basic themes of science. The Stan-dards speak to a "less is more" philosophy of science educa-tion which advocates present-ing a more focused content which allows teachers the op-portunity to address these top-ics in greater depth.

The eight categories of the Content Standards describe what all students should "know, understand and be able to do" as a result of expe-riencing science in the class-room. Together, the Content Standards define the breadth of the science content to be taught; but they do not pro-vide the organization for a sci-ence curriculum. That is left to us as teachers and to schools, curriculum designers, and communities. An effective curriculum provides empha-sis, balance, integration of content and detail, and addi-tional content when needed.

Content Standards de-scribe goals for student under-standing, not the instructional experiences through which our students will develop that un-derstanding. That is for the teachers and the school ad-ministrator to develop.

Standards Applicable to the Middle Level Grades

The first category of the Con-tent Standards, Unifying Concepts and Processes, ap-plies to grades K–12. The Na-tional Research Council presents the other seven categories, Standards A through G, in clusters for grades K–4, 5–8, and 9–12. (For a list of all the National Science Education Standards, see Appendix B.)

In this section, you will find examples of how some of the topics in the Standards might be taught at the middle level. Because middle level teachers are mindful of the preparation that their students have received in the elementary grades and concerned about the skills and knowledge that their students will need to be successful in high school, the *Middle Level Pathways* provides them with a roadmap of the standards showing the progression of topics across the K–12 span. Each of the content sections opens with a table that shows how content themes are developed across the grade levels.

This table is highlighted in a section, Building Concep-

tual Bridges, which introduces each of the content standards. This section describes the key ideas included at each grade level and emphasizes the kinds of conceptual understanding to be developed at the middle level.

Next is a description of a Classroom in Action. This describes an actual middle level classroom working toward implementing Standards-based reforms. As you read these scenarios, you may say to yourself, "I do that in my classroom." Congratulations! You are well on the pathway to the Standards. These vignettes were not designed to present idealized classroom situations, but rather real teachers, working with real middle level students, in real schools with all of the opportunities and constraints that they entail.

The next section in each of the content Standards is

Exploring the Standard. This provides some background information about the standard, suggestions from practicing middle level science teachers about the kinds of difficulties and misconceptions that middle level students may have with the Standards and a few suggested activities that might spark some ideas for addressing these misconceptions and developing a deeper conceptual understanding.

In each content category you will find a list of Resources for the Road that illustrate teaching consistent with the spirit of the Standards. Many of these resources, including all those from *Science and Children* and *Science Scope,* will be accessible on the compact disc.

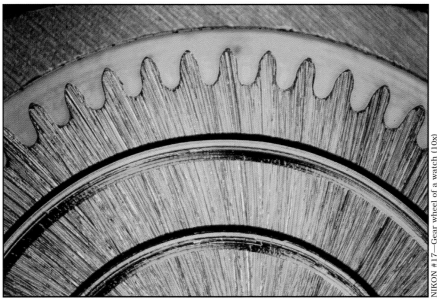

NIKON #17—Gear wheel of a watch (10x)

Conceptual and procedural schemes unify science disciplines and provide students with powerful ideas to help them understand the natural world. Because of the underlying principles embodied in this standard, the understandings and abilities described here are repeated in the other content standards. Unifying concepts and processes include

- *systems, order, and organization*
- *evidence, models, and explanation*
- *constancy, change, and measurement*
- *evolution and equilibrium*
- *form and function.*
  (NSES, page 104.)

In the literature of science education, it seems that great emphasis is placed on teaching process skills. But we know the reality is a blending of content and process. Perhaps when this is done well teachers move smoothly between the process of classification and the content of plant and animal characteristics. Measurement is not taught just for its own sake, but is used to record the action of forces on a moving body. Students engage in inquiry about a topic, and often, in the excitement of the inquiry, they learn more about the content than we would ever have imagined.

There are some concepts and processes that are so fundamental to science that they seem to cross this content-process dichotomy naturally. Back in the 1960s, educational reform movements ushered in a new approach to science teaching. The *Science: A Process Approach* (SAPA) curriculum of the American Association for the Advancement of Science promoted science process skills, such as observing, classifying, measuring, and predicting, as the organizing frameworks for teaching science. The logic behind this approach was that students needed to experience science in much the same way as practicing scientists do. The basic methodology was inquiry-based, in which students carried out investigations that focused on process skills.

About the same time, another curriculum, the *Science Curriculum Improvement Study* (SCIS) advocated a thematic approach. Its program was divided into two one-semester packages: life science and physical and Earth sciences. The grade-level units were based on broad themes of science, such as the properties of matter, interaction and systems, subsystems and variables, and scientific models.

Since the 1960s, many of the traditional textbook science curriculum materials have continued the traditional, discipline-based approach. Thematic science instruction has been kept alive by some innovative curriculum projects such as FOSS (Full Option Science Study), GEMS (Great Explorations in Mathematics and Science), and the Biological Sciences Curriculum Study (BSCS) Middle School program.

More recently, as the Standards advocate, there has been a movement toward "less is more" in the school science curriculum to counteract overloading the curriculum with every new fact and concept, fad, and trend. For years, teaching has focused more on "mentioning" the concepts of science rather than on developing deep understandings. Now science educators advocate identifying the key ideas of science and teaching them in depth.

Unlike the other content standards, the Unifying Concepts and Processes address all grade levels, K–12. The themes of this standard are fundamental and span all science disciplines. It is assumed that science teachers will address all the Unifying Concepts and Processes at appropriate levels of complexity in all science classes at all grade levels. Middle school students will be able to understand these concepts and processes to varying degrees. Most of them will have difficulty with the sequential ordering of events and they may find that understanding order at the cosmic level is perplexing. They may also find that the concept of system (the interrelationship of objects to form a whole) to be complex because it involves multiple variables. Middle school students are often very literal in their understanding of models, treating them as actual rather than conceptual representations of the world.

The Unifying Concepts and Processes give us a unique opportunity to focus students' attention on the grand ideas of science. In so doing, they invite students to experience the excitement of discovery that is fundamental to the nature of science.

PHOTODISC

MYRNA ROBLES

The Scientific Method

In my class, the students were learning about the scientific method. I noticed that they often had difficulty distinguishing between observations (information gained through the senses) and generalizations (statements that describe how or why a set of data behave as they do). In order to help them understand this better, I planned the following activity.

Identifying a common misconception that middle school students have.

I divided the class into pairs of students and gave each pair a small, cardboard box filled with two objects. Each of the boxes contained a different set of objects that were randomly selected from the storeroom. Some of the objects in the boxes included rubber and cork stoppers, a penny, a marble, and a large paper clip.

Focused on an example that used concrete materials.

"For the next few minutes, I want you to make some observations about the objects in your box. Record each observation as well as the sense (hearing, seeing, touching, tasting, smelling) that you used to make the observation. Because this box is sealed, most of your observations will be by hearing."

Students are encouraged to expand their senses beyond the obvious one of seeing.

The students went to work shaking and rolling, tilting and listening to the objects in their box.

"What are some of the observations that you made?" I asked. After a class discussion, I asked another question, "Do you think all of the boxes have the same objects? ("No.") What evidence do you have?" I listed the students' responses on the chalkboard. Do you all have the same number of objects?" ("Yes.")

"Now I would like you to make a statement about which objects you think are in your box. When you have made a decision, put a check mark by the observations that support your idea. For example, if you said that you heard two objects "clanging" as they hit, that might support the idea that there are two metal objects in the box."

When the teacher asks the students to provide a conclusion or an inference like "Do you think all of the boxes have the same objects?", he follows up the question immediately by asking students to provide the evidence for that conclusion.

I walked around while the students worked and encouraged them to add more inferences by asking questions such as, "What else do you think is in the box?" "What is your evidence?" "Do you think the objects are hard or soft?" "How do you know that?"

When they had completed their work, I engaged the class in a discussion of the differences between observations and generalizations. I pointed out that when students listed the evidence that they had obtained ("I heard two objects clink together," "I felt a heavy object rolling") that they were making observations. When they make statements about what objects were in the box, they were making generalizations. Finally, the students opened the boxes to see how well they had done.

George Serkin, *6th grade science teacher*

As a simple assessment, the teacher provided his students with statements, both observations and generalizations, and asked them to distinguish between the two.

MAX-KARL WINKLER

Systems, Order, and Organization

Systems, Order, and Organization are fundamental unifying concepts for understanding the nature of science. Science is based on the idea that there is order in the universe and that therefore the universe is predictable. Although random events occur in nature, it is the predictability (for example, forecasting weather) that makes science useful. The notion of cause and effect is basic to the experimental process. Middle school students will begin to understand cause and effect as it is described by Newton's Laws of Motion, by chemical reactions, the behavioral responses of organisms, and the geological cycles, just to name a few.

Organization means applying logical thinking about the world to uncover identifiable patterns (i.e., the periodic table, classification of organisms). Educational psychologists, such as Jean Piaget, believe that our search for order and organization is one of the strongest driving forces for learning. Trying to make sense out of the overwhelming amount of information available to us makes us want to organize our world. Your students will learn concepts of organization as they consider the similarity of the structure and function of living organisms, the role of different organisms in balancing ecosystems, and the charac-

FREDDIE BEA JOLIVETTE

teristics of different celestial bodies.

Perhaps the broadest of these three concepts is that of System. To understand the complexity of our world, we tend to consider smaller units or systems. A system refers to a group of components or parts that operate together in a coordinated manner to form some larger whole. Systems exist in all disciplines of science, including ecosystems, the solar system, and machines. Middle school students will confront many systems, including physical models of energy transfer, living systems, and the Earth as a global system.

Research suggests that young children believe that something is a system only when the parts are interacting in some active manner, and that changing the parts of a system by taking something away or adding something to it does not affect the system. Even in the middle grades, many of your students will have difficulty separating

the parts of the system from the nature of the overall system. They believe that the system as a whole is identical to its parts. For example, students see the solar system as the planets, the moons, and the sun rather than perceiving that the system includes the interactions of these bodies with one another.

You can help your students develop an understanding of this relationship through a variety of instructional experiences such as:

- observing weather patterns, air pressure, and temperatures over a period of time and predicting the weather for the future.

- observing the behavior of an organism, such as a goldfish, as it responds to environmental stimuli and developing a generalization to describe the organism's response.

- developing a classification scheme for a group of objects, such as a collection of leaves.

Your students will need numerous experiences in predicting future events and in observing patterns in their surroundings. They will also need the opportunity to observe the behavior of living and non-living systems that include random variability, such as the response of organisms to environmental stimuli, so they recognize that science is based on probabilities. For examples, you might give your students the opportunity to observe the reaction of brine shrimp to light and dark. Although the majority of the brine shrimp are attracted to the light, not all will be. Middle school students need to recognize that some organisms behave contrary to expectations and that these random fluctuations do not contradict general principles.

Evidence, Models, and Explanations

Observations are data gathered by our senses. Scientists generate new questions and obtain data by making observations. Evidence refers to specific observations and data that are used for scientific explanations. By the middle school, students should be well practiced at making observations, but they often have difficulty understanding which observations are most relevant to the problem at hand. For example, in studying the motion of a pendulum, your students may focus on the mass of the pendulum as the factor that influences its motion rather than the length of the pendulum.

Once scientists gather data, they make generalizations about them. Generalizations are statements about patterns in the data. These generalized explanations might be called hypotheses, models, laws, theories, or paradigms. Your students will be challenged constantly by these generalizations as they study Newton's Laws of Mo-

MICHAEL KELLY

tion, the Law of Conservation of Matter, the Law of Conservation of Energy, and the Theory of Evolution.

Models are a particular type of generalization that attempt to explain the real world. They may be: mathematical, such as an equation to describe the growth of a population; physical, like a scale model airplane to demonstrate principles of flight; or conceptual, such as using an analogy of water flow to describe the flow of electricity. Models explain the world but are not a substitute for the actual conditions of the world. It is important to impress upon your students that models are a representation of the world. As with any representation, something is lost in the attempt to simplify and explain. The computer is particularly useful in

developing and displaying models that can be changed easily to demonstrate the influences of new variables.

Models are a useful way of teaching concepts that cannot be experienced directly because
- they are primarily conceptual, such as atomic structure or electron flow.
- action takes place over long time spans, as with some concepts of evolution or as in erosion processes that formed of the Grand Canyon.
- the scale cannot be replicated in the classroom, such as volcanic eruptions or global energy cycles.

Students at this age are very literal. If you show them a model as a concrete representation, you need to distinguish clearly between those

BRUCE THOMAS

uid. At this point, their inferences should be refined with the new information.

In teaching about models, it is important to point out that all models fall short of describing the real world completely. For example, meteorologists have developed models of hurricane behavior. However, those models do not take into account all the variables that affect the motion of hurricanes. That is why the model does not predict the landfall of hurricanes with 100 percent accuracy.

The following activity uses easily obtained materials. Provide your class with containers of a clear, colorless, carbonated liquid, such as 7-UP™ or Sprite™, and some raisins. Then have your students place the raisins in the water. The raisins will begin rising and falling in the liquid. Ask the students to develop a model to explain the behavior of the raisins. You can expand the activity by asking the students to create a fictitious object that would be the best possible sinker or floater.

Constancy, Change, and Measurement

Much of what we know to be science is a search for understanding the process of change. The early alchemists, considered by some to be pre-scientists, were driven to find

parts of the model that are relevant to the phenomena you are trying to describe and those that are not.

Many of the concepts associated with a topic will be difficult for middle level students to understand, especially those who are cognitively at the concrete operational stage. Your students will have difficulty making mental constructs of novel ideas, such as creating a model to explain a set of data. They will be helped by representing their explanations, or models in written, verbal, pictorial, or concrete models whenever possible.

In addition, your students will need numerous opportunities to make observations. Often middle school students have difficulty distinguishing between observations and inferences. For example, if they are shown an orange-colored liquid, students might say, "It's orange juice" (an inference) rather than "It is an orange colored liquid." Inferences that are not based upon observations are guesses, and are not scientific.

As one activity, you might provide your students with a mystery liquid. The acid-base indicator bromothymol blue is commonly used because it changes from blue to yellow-green when air is blown through a drinking straw into the liquid. The addition of carbon dioxide makes a weak solution of carbonic acid and lowers the pH of the liquid. Have your students make numerous observations of the liquid. They may jump to conclusions about the identity of the liquid ("It's Windex," or "It's grape juice"). They will observe the color change as a result of blowing into the liq-

the philosopher's stone that could change base metals into gold. Modern science and technology is similarly motivated to trying to understand our constantly changing world. Examples include: changes in the human body, like growth, disease, and aging; geological processes, such as earthquakes, weathering, and geological cycles; changes in physical properties, like chemical change, physical changes, force, and motion. Much as scientists focus on change, they are even more excited when they discover a constant. Some consider the conservation laws, such as conservation of mass or energy, to be among the most important principles in science.

Change has three properties: magnitude, direction, and rate. The magnitude refers to the size of the change. The direction, although most commonly described as a cardinal direction (north, south, east, and west), is broadened to include a positive or negative change, as in health or illness. The rate refers to how fast the change is taking place. All of these properties require measurement in order to characterize the change. The metric system is most commonly used by scientists. Certainly by the middle school years, students need frequent opportunities to make metric measurements of length, volume, mass, and temperature. Students also need to understand that different measure-

ment systems are used for different purposes.

Rate involves the comparison of two quantities. Most often one of these quantities is time, such as kilometers per hour. Because rate involves the comparison of two dynamic, changing variables, it can be a very difficult concept for middle school students to understand.

Much research has been conducted on students' understanding of the conservation of numbers, length and area, terms used by Jean Piaget to refer to the ability of a child to recognize that two groups of objects are the same even when they are displayed in different ways. This meaning should not be confused with the conservation of mass or energy as used in Physical science. Although most middle school students should have an understanding of the conservation of number, length, and area, some of your students will have difficulty with the conservation of weight and displaced volume. Density is associated with most of these ideas and it is not surprising that many middle school students find density to be a particularly difficult concept to grasp, even after having hands-on experiences with density problems. In addition, students through high school have difficulty translating motion into graphical representations. According to the American Association for the Advancement of Science, "The goal for all Americans

should be modest: to understand a graph of any familiar variable against time in terms of reading it and interpreting its ups and downs in a story about what is going on. Eventually, steepness as well as direction of change can become part of the story."

You can help your students to understand these concepts by providing them with many opportunities to observe and record change. Starting at the lower middle grades, students are able to observe phenomena such as the germination of seeds, and record change on a daily basis. As they progress in maturity, they can begin to consider more abstract changes such as changes in geological landforms, in chemical systems, and in metabolic processes. These abstract changes may need to be modeled, and it is important that students are provided with many concrete experiences (for example, manipulating cut-outs of the continents to understand plate tectonics).

Students also need the opportunity to make scale models (of geological time, of the solar system, etc.) in order to understand the processes that take place on scales greater than that which they can experience personally. A common activity is for students to use a strip of adding machine tape to portray the distances of the planets from the Sun using a scale model.

Evolution and Equilibrium

Evolution refers to biological, geological, or astronomical change over time. It may even refer to the evolution of technology (such as the change in the computer from room-sized to pocket-sized). The changes of an organism over millions of years to adapt itself better to the environment, the uplift of great mountain ranges, the birth and death of solar systems are all examples of evolution. Evolution differs from change in that it has direction and shows a progression that can be traced from one form to another over time.

The California Science Framework identified three subthemes related to evolution: direction, constraints, and chance. Direction means that events are influenced by what happened before. These prior events constrain evolution, as does the environment. Still, underlying all of evolution is the chance event—the random gene mutation, the catastrophic event—that can serve as a trigger for change.

Counterbalancing evolution is equilibrium. This is a condition that is reached when opposing forces are balanced. The natural world tends toward equilibrium because the energy required to maintain equilibrium is generally less than that needed to initiate change. For example, middle school students will

learn that heat moves from warmer objects to colder objects until they both reach the same temperature. They will also learn that the body has many mechanisms to maintain a state of equilibrium or health. It is when these mechanisms break down—a cut in the skin, for example—that disease can result.

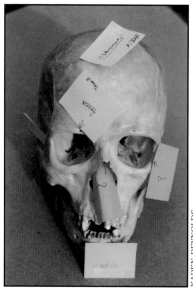

KAREN REYNOLDS

A difficulty that students will have with this concept is the scale of time over which evolutionary changes occur. Most evolutionary changes are subtle unless observed over the period of many generations. Because of this, your students will have difficulty conceptualizing the scale of time involved in the evolutionary process. In addition, geological evolution occurs on a grand scale. Again, this will be difficult for many middle school students to understand. Models may be helpful in providing an example for a process that the students can-

not visualize, but care must be taken that the model, by simplifying the global process, doesn't introduce additional misconceptions.

Because of the difficulty that students will have understanding the time scale involved in evolution, a useful activity is to ask your students to create geological time scale by using a roll of adding machine tape. Your students can record significant geological and biological events at this scale as well as the brief period occupied by historical events which will lead naturally to an interdisciplinary connection. One thing that they will notice immediately is that the emergence of humans on Earth is a recent event.

There are rapidly reproducing organisms that are commercially available and will allow your students to observe changes over time from one generation to another. Plants, like the Wisconsin Fast Plants or organisms that reproduce rapidly, such as fruit flies, allow students to observe the effects of random gene mutations on organisms.

Form and Function

Form and function are two closely related concepts both in the natural and the designed world. The form of a bone is related to its function whether that be the honeycombed structure of the bones of a bird's wing that provide strength and minimize weight, or the thick bones of an elephant's leg designed to support huge weights. The design of a building is dictated by aesthetics, and by the purpose that the building is to serve. The form of a moving object (whether on wheels or sliding) will influence the efficiency of its function under varying situations.

A fundamental concept of evolution is the way that form has changed over time to accommodate changes in function. Consider the way in which bridge designs have changed to accommodate the weight of cars and trucks.

Thinking simultaneously about form and function may be difficult for many of your middle school students. Their orientation has been typical on either the form of an object (the aesthetics of a sculpture) or the function (the purpose of a pair of scissors). There are numerous examples from the designed world of the blending of form and function to create objects that are both functional and aesthetic (think of some of the great examples of architecture).

You can provide many opportunities for your students to explore form and function. Some possibilities that might interest middle school students include the following:

- give your students a common object (for example, a 35mm film canister) and asked them to create new ways of using it.
- consider homology in the structure of organisms. How are the leg bones and skulls of horses similar to those of humans? How do the different functions of the bones of these two organisms relate to differences in the form of the bones?
- extend the concept of form and function into the designed world by looking at architecture. The books by David McCauley are particularly helpful in illustrating these concepts.
- have an "invention convention" in which students design new products using only recycled objects or materials. This challenges students to consider new functions for common materials.

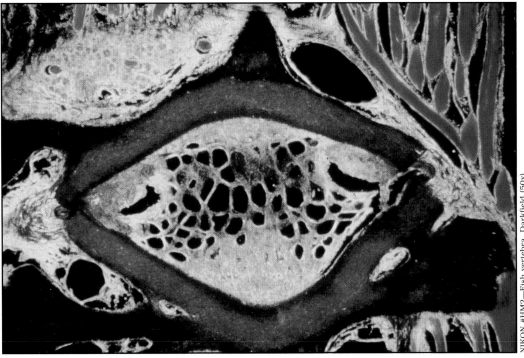

NIKON #HM2—Fish vertebra. Darkfield (50x)

Comparison of K–12 NSES Content Standard A: Science as Inquiry

The complete text for the Standard related to Science as Inquiry is found in NSES. Each part of the Standard discussed below is identified by its highlighted main statement.

Levels K–4	Levels 5–8	Levels 9–12
ABILITIES NECESSARY TO DO SCIENTIFIC INQUIRY	**ABILITIES NECESSARY TO DO SCIENTIFIC INQUIRY**	**ABILITIES NECESSARY TO DO SCIENTIFIC INQUIRY**
• Ask a question about objects, organisms, and events in the environment.	• Ask questions that can be answered through scientific investigations.	• Identify questions and concepts that guide scientific investigations.
• Plan and conduct a simple investigation.	• Design and conduct a scientific investigation.	• Design and conduct scientific investigations.
• Employ simple equipment and tools to gather data and extend the senses.	• Use appropriate tools and techniques to gather, analyze, and interpret data. • Use mathematics in all aspects of scientific inquiry.	• Use technology and mathematics to improve investigations and communications.
• Use data to construct a reasonable explanation.	• Develop descriptions, explanations, predictions, and models using evidence.	• Formulate and revise scientific explanations and models using logic and evidence.
	• Recognize and analyze alternative explanations and predictions.	• Recognize and analyze alternative explanations and models.
• Communicate investigations and explanations.	• Communicate scientific procedures and explanations.	• Communicate and defend a scientific argument.
	• Think critically and logically to develop the relationship between evidence and explanation.	
UNDERSTANDING ABOUT SCIENTIFIC INQUIRY	**UNDERSTANDING ABOUT SCIENTIFIC INQUIRY**	**UNDERSTANDING ABOUT SCIENTIFIC INQUIRY**
• Investigations in science involve asking questions, finding answers, and comparing the unknown to the known.	• The relationship of the different types of questions to the kinds of scientific investigations.	• Question how systems work, how conceptual principles guide scientific knowledge, and how historical and current scientific knowledge affect scientific inquiry.
• Different ways to investigate.	• Effect of current scientific knowledge on scientific investigations. Different approaches used to advance knowledge.	• Reasons for conducting scientific investigations.
• Use of instruments such as magnifiers, thermometers, timers, and other devices for measuring and observing.	• Value of technology in science.	• Reliance on technology.
	• Importance of mathematics.	• Mathematics is essential in scientific inquiry.
• Scientific explanations from evidence (observations) and scientific knowledge (what is already known about the world).	• Characteristics of scientific explanations. Process of displacement of ideas by better explanations.	• Criteria for scientific explanations.
• Communicate the results of investigations to others.		• Communicate results of scientific inquiry, report methodology, defend results logically to enable further investigation.
• Scientists question the work of other scientists.	• Value and practice skepticism, questioning, evaluation, and suggesting alternatives in making scientific advances.	
	• There are multiple outcomes to scientific investigations.	

A comparison of the Standard for Science as Inquiry for K–4, 5–8, and 9–12 grades shows that students at the middle level use their investigative abilities with more sophistication, and develop a better appreciation of investigative processes and tools than they did at the elementary level. For example, middle level students generate questions just as students in grades K–4 do, but they also learn to identify those that are appropriate for investigation, an important step toward understanding the function of questions in designing investigations in the future at the high school level.

Middle level students have a better grasp of relevant evidence and valid arguments. As they exercise their newfound powers of critical thinking, they engage in skepticism and begin to question information previously taken on faith. The use of mathematics allows them to distinguish between qualitative and quantitative information, develop a greater precision in measurements, and improve their logical thinking.

When middle level students engage in focused investigations, they discover relationships by making observations and by the systematic gathering of data. A working understanding of fractions develops an understanding of concepts such as pressure as a ratio of force to area rather than a push-force, speed as a measurable rate over distance, and proportions as representations of constant relationships. These students can interpret graphs that show changes over time or one measurement as a function of another.

While students in lower grades carry out simple experiments and often understand a fair test, middle level students are able to understand the reasons for controlling variables better as they begin to identify and understand cause-and-effect relationships. Certain tendencies may persist, such as basing conclusions on single occurrences and placing value on results when variables have either no effect or an opposite effect. However, with experience and time, students can compensate for these shortcomings.

A middle level program rich in investigative experience prepares students for the more complex challenges to come at the high school level.

PHOTODISC

Casting Pewter Jewelry

The hand holding the pan is protected by a glove. The propane torch keeps the metal in a molten state as it is poured into the molds.

When my eighth graders came to science from art class, they were very excited about an upcoming special week-long session in making pewter jewelry. The process, they explained, would include making their own individual "cool" designs; carving the designs into soft plaster of Paris to make molds; pouring molten metal into the molds, allowing the piece to harden; and refining their work by filing and polishing, and adding pin backs, ear ring wires, or chains if they wanted them. Since I had had a conversation with the art teacher about the project several weeks earlier, I was ready—ready to be enthusiastic about the great news and ready with some science to support the experience. So, I asked them to tell me more—such as, "What is pewter, anyway?" "Why did the art teacher choose pewter instead of some other metal?" "Is it safe?" (An amalgam without lead was used for this project.) "How does the mold work—doesn't everything stick together?" "What special tools will be used?" "What is the history of this technology?" There was an enthusiastic response to the suggestion that we shift our classwork into an investigation of some of the science behind this art project, the kind of science and technology that artists need to know when they carry out this kind of creative work.

In preparation for our investigation, and possible spin-off investigations, we listed questions we wanted to answer and clustered them around science topics and concepts. These included the following:

Characteristics of matter:

What are the characteristics of plaster of Paris that make it useful for this project?

What is pewter made of?

What are its characteristics?

Why does it make good jewelry?

Teachers from different subject areas can collaborate.

Questioning strategies serve to focus thinking and prompt curiosity.

Motivation is built in when students take ownership in deciding what to study in science, whether by generating ideas or selecting from various choices.

Making connections between activities, related questions, and science content serves as an advance organizer for the students, providing an overview of what we can do and what to expect.

Which designs will not break?

Physical changes:
How can the shape of pewter be controlled?
What are all the materials used, and which are used to change others? (Refer to scratching, carving, filing, or melting.)

Heat energy:
How do we protect ourselves from being burned by the heat?
How does heat travel and cause physical changes like melting and solidifying?

Safety and tool technology:
What are the safety precautions for this project?
What tools are used? How are they designed for specific uses?
During the next two weeks the students engaged in science activities that complemented and coincided with the art project, which started during the second week of science and continued one additional week. The art teacher and I compared notes frequently in order to avoid redundancy and to reinforce concepts for each other. During the first week, students mixed plaster of Paris into blocks. At a computer station equipped with a temperature probe, one team of students plotted the change of temperature effected by the exothermic reaction between the dry plaster and water. Students were able to view the process and the results. All students, working in teams, tested different proportions of water to plaster to see how the results would differ in strength and time it took for the plaster to solidify. The importance of recording amounts and times carefully was stressed, since the "best recipe" would be important for everyone to know. Group work, including lab clean-up responsibilities, allowed students to collaborate in all parts of the investigations of the plaster of Paris. Results were published (posted on the wall) so that comparisons could be made and student teams could consult with each other. Once determined, this recipe was used to make blocks that would be cut in half in the art class and carved out for molds. During follow-up class discussion, I made comparisons between the setting and curing of the plaster with that of concrete. Students contributed additional activities, such as preparing molds to make false teeth.

Remaining activities during the two weeks included (1) background fact finding, (2) a review of heat energy and physical changes, and (3) a focus on tools and technology. Safety was addressed in the art class.

1. All students engaged in searching for information on the Web and other sources to find out about famous and contemporary sculptors specializing in metal casting, technology of metal casting, and famous works of art produced by metal casting. Extended time was provided for a specialist team to gather the results of the searches, digitized photos of the students making their own pewter jewelry, and statements by the student "artists" in order to produce a multimedia presentation that accompanied a public display of the jewelry.

Experience with concepts in different contexts benefits learning.

Using a computer to gather, organize, and display data for interpretation is an effective way to use new technology.

Controlling variables and maintaining careful records are part of Standard A.

Limited resources can be shared by setting up demonstration or display stations.

Communication was carried out in a variety of ways. Effective communication had consequences for peers.

Group work and intergroup interaction allows discussion that is essential for clarification of ideas.

Producing results that will be applied elsewhere adds credibility to the effort.

Examples of similar phenomena with familiar materials benefits concept understanding.

New avenues for demonstrating knowledge also promote technology literacy.

MAX-KARL WINKLER

2. Basic to understanding metal casting is the control of metal in its liquid and solid forms. The physics of heat energy and its relation to this process in jewelry making were presented in the science class through videos, an exploration with melting and casting candle wax, and testing various materials for heat conductivity.

Opportunities are provided for individuals or groups to participate in specialized activities.

3. Tools and materials, such as torches, crucibles, tongs, heat protective gloves, files, plaster of Paris, glue, pewter, and other materials were considered for their special characteristics and functions. The students inspected the collection, borrowed from the art class for two days, adopted the items individually or in pairs, prepared a descriptive card to serve as "museum signage," and produced a short run display of jewelry making technology. The multimedia photo team took advantage of the opportunity to capture images, and the display was visited by several classes of seventh graders. An activity associated with tools used for carving the plaster and filing the metal was extended to an investigation of the relative hardness of a variety of materials and the use of Moh's scale to quantify results of tests.

The power of cooperation is demonstrated through efforts in which each individual contributes to a constructive project in a significant way.

Students reported that they enjoyed the interdisciplinary nature of the classwork and appreciated the amount of science that artists should know. They were assessed in a variety of ways, including participation in discussion, oral and written reports of searches, displays, products, investigation summaries, interviews, special projects, and evidence of transfer of scientific knowledge to practice in the art studio. I especially enjoyed the collaboration with a colleague and felt that the students were able to use, or at least reflect on, their learning from science in the authentic context of the jewelry casting project in their art class.

Students are given different kinds of opportunities to demonstrate success in learning.

Connecting concepts to authentic experience is an essential element of the constructivist learning environment.

Ms. C.J. Brown-Ejuko, *7th and 8th grade science teacher*

Introduction to Exploring

As we incorporate the Standard for Science as Inquiry into our thinking and planning, it is useful to review the content coverage, identify ways to help students develop understanding, challenge misconceptions, consider applications in various fields of science, and make connections with other subject areas.

MYRNA ROBLES

Abilities Necessary to Do Scientific Inquiry

Identify questions that can be answered by conducting scientific investigations (NSES, page 145).

Some questions can be addressed through objective investigations while others involve matters that are not objective by nature or involve other processes, such as moral reflection. Students should be encouraged to raise questions about the world around them, but they will need assistance in identifying subjects that can be tested scientifically and in distinguishing them from issues that are by their nature subjective. Some students at this level may appreciate the characteristics that distinguish science from literature, religion, and the arts. In addition, students can learn to distinguish between science-based

technology that *supports* fields like the visual arts, music, politics, and communications, and the specific *content* of those fields. For example, science contributes to the understanding of the composition of pigments used by artists. The resulting technology provides a choice of many hues for the painter. However, science does not explain how the colors in a painting are appreciated aesthetically.

Design and conduct a scientific investigation (NSES, page 145).

Middle level students should:
* use general abilities to clarify questions for investigation
* design ways to gather information about what is known
* identify and control variables, gather and organize observations and other data
* interpret data
* use evidence to construct explanations

* consider and propose alternate explanations.

Most students, at least in the beginning, cannot carry out all stages of an investigation independently. Challenges to "choose anything you want to do and do it" usually precipitate high levels of frustration and often lead to outside adult intervention, resulting in the students being accused of "not doing it themselves." Teachers can facilitate success by
* providing guidelines or boundaries within which to explore
* assisting students in choosing between interesting questions
* monitoring design plans
* providing relevant examples of effective observation and organization strategies
* checking and improving skills in the use of instruments, technology, and techniques

- making students aware of models that can serve as references or resources.

In a constructivist environment, student-centered experience that leads to an understanding of investigative processes and the concepts within the science content, involves constant interaction between students and the teacher for feedback, confirmation, redirection, clarification, and affirmation. Collaboration, discussion, clarification, debate, explanation, and critique are important parts of learning science through social interaction.

Use appropriate tools and techniques to gather, analyze, and interpret data (NSES, page 145).

Middle level students are prepared to use a variety of tools, instruments, and techniques to gather, analyze, and interpret data. They are able to differentiate between qualitative and quantitative information and, with help, appreciate the appropriateness of each in relation to the investigative contexts. When exploring a phenomenon or testing general hypotheses, qualitative data may be sufficient, although in other cases quantitative results are needed to identify more specific relationships and compare data from different trials.

In addition to using a variety of measuring instruments, students should have experience with instruments that vary in levels of accuracy. Household scales and the triple beam balance each have their strengths and limitations as instruments for measuring mass, and when each is used appropriately, it can be very useful in investigations.

Students should be aware of the appropriate application of techniques, such as those used for sampling; they should consider the effects of the misuse of sampling strategies. For example, when an investigation involves interacting with people, it is important, but not always easy, for students to distinguish between gathering data that represent opinions and data that are merely descriptive.

The development of new or more powerful sensing devices and other technology, and of computers which can receive and process large amounts of information in very short periods of time, has extended the ability of scientists to explore areas that were not accessible before. Students can also use computer-based instruments to gather data remotely or as extensions of the senses. Computers can be used to manage, organize and display data for simple statistical analysis. It is important that experience with tools and techniques for gathering, analyzing, and interpreting data be embedded in authentic contexts, as part of actual investigations carried out by the

students. These experiences should include direct measurements and data collection by the students as well as finding and using data collected by others. Classwork can be directly connected to larger projects accessible through the Internet or other means.

Develop descriptions, explanations, predictions, and models using evidence (NSES, page 145).

Determining what is and is not relevant information can be a fairly sophisticated process. Students need practice in describing and explaining their own observations as well as evidence provided by other sources. Keeping logs and journals helps students learn to differentiate between descriptions and explanations. When applying knowledge, students should distinguish between a guess and a prediction, basing predictions on relevant information.

Students develop new knowledge for themselves when they make connections between the evidence they gather through their own observations and the main body of knowledge accumulated by science. Teachers should facilitate extensive and varied experiences that allow students to examine enough evidence to develop logical descriptions, explanations, predictions, and models.

Think critically and logically to

make the relationships between evidence and explanations (NSES, page 145).

Distinguishing between useful and irrelevant information is not always easy for the middle level student. When carrying out investigations and gathering information, students must recognize which evidence should be used in identifying relationships and constructing explanations, and how to account for nonrelevant evidence.

Students should understand why controlling variables is essential when establishing and confirming cause-and-effect relationships. They should distinguish between evidence that supports correlations and evidence that supports a cause-and-effect relationship. Explanations should be constructed logically and changed when new evidence cannot be accommodated by existing explanations. Students' understanding develops best when they experience multiple investigations in which they discuss and challenge ideas that have a level of complexity appropriate for their level of cognitive development. Teachers can help students become aware of the processes by promoting and reinforcing thinking that is critical and logical. Useful questions:

- Does that explanation really make sense?
- Why does that explanation make sense?
- Why does this line of thinking not satisfy me?
- What can we say to support

CAROL WILLIAMSON

this idea and what does not support it?
- What can we do about evidence that cannot be accounted for?
- Could there be another reason?
- Is that an observation or an opinion?
- How did we get here from there?

Students do not necessarily like to relinquish their first explanations. The process of thinking through ideas and changing explanations must be made rewarding.

Recognize and analyze alternative explanations and predictions (NSES, page 148).

When students discover one answer, we are challenged to keep them engaged in the inquiry process long enough to consider alternatives. To this end, it is important to establish an environment in which multiple possibilities are considered; this process is as important as arriving at the final result.

Students are often asked to express their views or opinions about which of several possibilities are the most logical. This often results in a kind of "vote" and commitment to the most popular response. It is important that students feel safe in expressing ideas and thoughts that might be minority views. Also, students should follow up scientific investigation with testing, not politicking, to determine logical explanations. In the real world, scientists differ in the explanations and conclusions they reach from the same set of data and observations. This usually leads to additional observations, new analysis, and a review of the conditions under which the tests were conducted, producing even more carefully considered explanations. In this way differences of opinion between scientists can lead to better science.

Communicate scientific procedures and explanations (NSES, page 148).

The importance of accurate and clearly communicated records and reports cannot be overstated. Consider the following situations:
- a field biologist returns to a location to measure the growth of individual plants he observed five years ago.
- a geologist checks previous records of erosion rates in a particular valley in order to assess changes that have occurred over the last 150 years. She also compares

her current observations with the geologic record.

- a scientist must leave a research project investigating several viruses very suddenly and is replaced by another researcher who continues the project.
- a scientist questions the validity of conclusions from research carried out by a famous scientist 50 years ago.
- astronomers use existing data to develop plans for new technology that allows them to probe deeper into space.
- a student is asked to reanalyze his data to answer a new question that he had not asked when he designed and carried out his initial investigation.

In each case careful communication of the scientific procedures, records, and explanations are essential for maintaining continuity in scientific work. Errors in the recording process can mislead scientific effort and cause costly mistakes resulting in decisions that are based on faulty information. Students engaged in scientific endeavors are contributing to scientific knowledge when they communicate clearly for their own benefit and that of others. Practice in following directions and communicating the results of their own work should be carried out through writing, oral reports, drawings, diagrams, multimedia products, and other means.

Use mathematics in all aspects of scientific inquiry (NSES, page 148).

As investigations, questions, and problems in science become more extensive and complex, inquiry must incorporate the powerful tools of mathematics. Middle level students should grow to appreciate the use of mathematics for measuring, solving problems, perceiving and giving logical explanations of relationships, and providing models that use symbols. This is especially true when mathematics is linked to concrete activities and its application is generated directly from the desire to answer questions during scientific inquiry. Students should use mathematics in all appropriate forms, matching the use to the problem, and selecting strategies that fit the abilities of the students. This includes measurement (distances, time, angles, temperature, and other variables), geometry, fractions, simple equations, frequencies, rates, speed, conversions, and other mathematical constructs.

Understanding about Scientific Inquiry

Different kinds of questions suggest different kinds of scientific investigations (NSES, page 148).

An inquiring mind, curiosity, and the ability to apply critical

thinking to problems are basic to scientific inquiry. Carefully phrased questions will lead the students toward the scientific method of investigation.

Students should be allowed to ask questions, make observations, and ask more questions, thus refining the investigative process. How to ask a good science question should be part of every science class. Time spent on producing good questions is time well spent. The following are good science questions:

- What lives in a meadow?
- How does temperature affect snail behavior?
- Do potholes grow at a constant rate?
- How much of the Earth's surface experiences rainfall at any given time?
- How fast can a person's eyes adapt to the dark?
- Should orchards be saved from housing developments?

These questions can be addressed by scientific investigations, but each suggests a different approach. For example: surveys, observations, experiment under controlled conditions, measurement over time, monitoring of environmental conditions, gathering data available on the Internet, tests using improvised or standardized instruments and procedures, and fact gathering are useful approaches for students to build informed opinions. Although all use scientific methodology, not every investigation needs to be an experiment.

Science As Inquiry

Current scientific knowledge and understanding guide scientific investigations. Different scientific domains employ different methods, core theories, and standards to advance scientific knowledge and understanding (NSES, page 148).

Students should understand that scientific inquiry is carried out in many ways that are appropriate for the field of study and the investigative objectives. Science programs that provide experiences in all the major science disciplines (Earth, life, and physical science) each year for every student recognize that cognitive growth affects conceptual understanding in all scientific domains. Although certain tools and techniques are common to all the sciences, most fields have specialized tools and techniques with which students should become familiar. Investigations in the different fields provide such opportunities. A survey of a vacant lot or stream over several seasons introduces students to the methodology used in ecology and biology. A study of calories in food samples involves physics and chemistry. Tracking storms through the Internet can be connected to meteorology, climatology, and Earth systems. Raising fish involves controlling environmental effects and understanding specific reproductive and growth requirements.

Mathematics is important in all

PHOTO© 1998 CHRIS KUHLMAN/CK PRODUCTIONS

aspects of scientific inquiry (NSES, page 148).

Mathematics provides precision and efficient methods for comparing and compiling data. It has contributed significantly to most scientific progress for thousands of years and continues to be important in formulating convincing explanations.

Computers are available for making rapid calculations, organizing of data, and displaying relationships. Time can be saved by using computers to process data, leaving more time for interpreting, proposing relationships, theorizing, and evaluating the significance of the investigations. With computers and interfacing instruments, students are able to carry out many trials during an experiment. Computers also make it possible for middle level students to use simple statistics as a tool

for analysis. Connections between science and mathematics curricula are many, with science providing authentic contexts for applying mathematics skills.

Technology used to gather data enhances accuracy and allows scientists to analyze and quantify results of investigations (NSES, page 148).

Technology has allowed scientists to extend human senses and to gather data objectively on programmed schedules and in remote locations. Calculations are rapid and consistent so that more of the scientist's time can be spent for interpreting, proposing new problems or tests, analyzing, explaining, and theorizing. Quantified results allow scientists to make comparisons between different investigations, in different locations over a period of time. Technology now allows scientists to communicate instantly all over the world. Discussion and collaboration between scientists is no longer dependent on physical proximity.

Scientific explanations emphasize evidence, have logically consistent arguments, and use scientific principles, models, and theories. The scientific community accepts and uses such explanations until displaced by better scientific ones. When such displacement occurs, science advances (NSES, page 148).

New evidence, explanations, and reasoning give us the opportunity to change our minds and replace old ideas with new ones. Better understanding allows us to revisit old observations and gain new perspectives. Understanding that changing or clarifying explanations based on new evidence is fundamental in appreciating the difference between science and other disciplines. Scientific progress is built on a series of changes in understanding that are expected to continue to change. "A scientist's work is never done."

Science advances through legitimate skepticism. Asking questions and questioning other scientists' explanations are part of scientific inquiry. Scientists evaluate the explanations proposed by other scientists by examining evidence, comparing evidence, identifying faulty reasoning, pointing out statements that go beyond the evidence, and suggesting alternative explanations for the same observations (NSES, page 148).

Scientific habits of mind serve the citizen in daily life. Students become more sophisticated consumers when they see weaknesses in claims made by non-expert celebrities or unidentified "leading doctors..." or by demonstrations that lack controls. They begin to notice inappropriate comparisons and irrelevant evidence.

Because so much of scientific activity is spent in scrutinizing evidence and explanations, data that has been carefully recorded and communicated can be reviewed and revisited frequently, providing insights beyond the original investigative period or intent. This healthy indulgence in skepticism supports teaching and learning strategies that allow students to discuss, debate, question, explain, clarify, compare, and propose new thinking through social discourse.

Our challenge at the middle level, where students are beginning to exercise their right to be skeptics, is to draw the distinction between reacting to what others say and reacting to the persons themselves. Debate and disagreement in science still require diplomacy and objectivity. Developing a taste for the intellectual pursuits of science has long-term rewards for all students.

Scientific investigations sometimes result in new ideas and phenomena for study, generate new methods or procedures for an investigation, or develop new technologies to improve the collection of data. All of these results can lead to new investigations (NSES, page 148).

Students should value the variety of results associated with an investigative activity. Often the new questions that are generated are as important to the student as the results of the investigation. The history of science and technology has many examples of individuals who were sufficiently perceptive to recognize new ideas and made unexpected discoveries while performing routine work.

The TV and text series *Connections* by James Burke presents many intriguing links between investigations and innovations. Allowing students to improvise techniques for measuring, manipulating apparatus, and gathering data will help them to gain insight into the evolution of techniques and tools. Teachers should be prepared to recognize students' tangential successes as well as their planned achievements.

Baird, Hugh. (1994, November/December). Keying out Banana Splits. *Science Scope, 18* (3), 12–16.

Barry, Dana Malloy. (1990, September). Fat Burgers. *Science Scope, 14* (1), 34–36.

Cothron, Julia H., Giese, Ronald N., and **Rezba, Richard J.** (1993). *Students and Research: Practical Strategies for Science Classrooms and Competitions (2nd ed.).* Dubuque, IA: Kendall/Hunt Publishing.

Freedman, Robin Lee Harris, and **Roberts, Faimon.** (1995, November/December). How Sweet It Is. *Science Scope, 19* (3), 34–36.

Germann, Paul J., Aram, Roberta, and **Burke, Gerald.** (1996, January). Identifying Patterns and Relationships among the Responses of Seventh-Grade Students to the Science Process Skill of Designing Experiments. *Journal of Research in Science Teaching, 33* (1), 79–99.

Keys, Carolyn W. (1996, February). Inquiring Minds Want to Know. *Science Scope, 19* (5), 17–19.

McBride, John, and **Villanueva, Roy.** (1997, January). Salt Crystals: Exploring the Scientific Method. *Science Scope, 20* (4), 20–23.

Mesmer, Karen. (1996, September). Research in the Life Science Classroom. *Science Scope, 20* (1), 31–32.

Misiti, Frank, Jr. (1996, May). Keys to the Natural World. *Science Scope, 19* (8), 16–18.

Rakow, Steven J. (1986). *Teaching Science as Inquiry.* Bloomington, IN: Phi Delta Kappa Educational Foundation.

Schriver, Marti, David, Teresa, and **Stewart, Charlene.** (1997, March). Research—Mud, Bugs, and Fun. *Science Scope, 20* (6), 46–49.

Stiles, John R. (1992, November/December). Mealworms: A Year-Round Science Project. *Science Scope, 16* (3), 36–39.

Vega, Sharon. (1996, September). The Big Horn Mine: Digging Into the Scientific Method. *Science Scope, 20* (1), 12–14.

Williams, Lois E. (1996, January). Burning Questions About Candles. *Science Scope, 19* (4), 10–13.

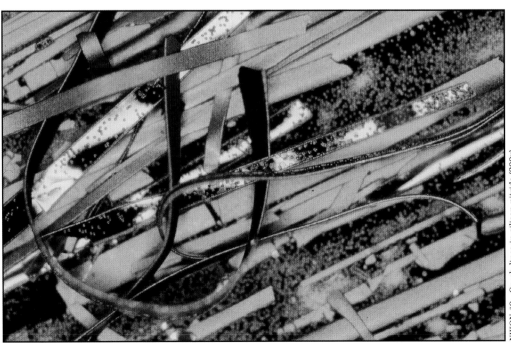

NIKON #9—Crush-lines in silicon nitride (200x)

Comparison of K–12 NSES Content Standard B: Physical Science

The complete text for the Standard related to Physical Science is found in NSES. Each part of the Standard discussed below is identified by its highlighted main statement.

LEVELS K–4	LEVELS 5–8	LEVELS 9–12
PROPERTIES OF OBJECTS AND MATERIALS	**PROPERTIES CHANGES OF PROPERTIES IN MATTER**	**STRUCTURE OF ATOMS AND PROPERTIES OF MATTER**
• Observe the properties of and measure objects.	• Characteristic properties of substances. Separating the components of mixtures.	• Electron sharing and chemical properties. • Elements and element families, the Periodic Table of Elements. • Atomic bonding. • Physical properties of compounds.
• Objects made of multiple combinations of properties.		• Carbon-based molecules • Molecular arrangements of solids, liquids and gases.
• Different states—gas, liquid, solid—and changes of state in common materials caused by heating and cooling.		
		CHEMICAL REACTIONS
	• Chemical reactions, grouping of substances with common chemical properties, and the conservation of mass. • Characteristics of chemical elements, their variety and the compounds that account for the living and nonliving substances we encounter.	• Occurrence of chemical reactions. • Kinds of chemical reactions. • Time periods for chemical reactions. • Catalysts.
		STRUCTURE OF ATOMS
		• Atomic and subatomic makeup of matter. • Isotopes. • The nucleus. • Radioactive isotopes. • Energy release and consumption.
POSITION AND MOTION OF OBJECTS	**MOTIONS AND FORCES**	**MOTIONS AND FORCES**
• Describe the positions of objects. • Describe the motion of objects. • Changing the positions and motion of objects relating to the push or pull.	• Describe the position, direction of motion, and speed of an object. Graphing motion and Inertia. • Effect of multiple forces on the movement, speed, and direction of an object.	• Laws of motion. • Laws of gravitational attraction. • Laws of electrical charges. • Relation between observable forces and molecular electric forces. • Electromagnetic force.
• Sounds produced by vibrating objects. Changing the pitch of sound.		
LIGHT, HEAT, ELECTRICITY, AND MAGNETISM	**TRANSFER OF ENERGY**	**CONSERVATION OF ENERGY AND INCREASE IN DISORDER**
• Properties of light including straight line of travel, reflection, refraction, and absorption. • Heat production and conduction.	• Light transmission, absorption, and scattering. How we see an object.	
	• Heat moves from a warmer object to a cooler one, until both reach the same temperature.	• Heat as random motion.
	• Energy transfer.	• Transfer of energy.
• Electricity in circuits to produce light, heat, sound, and magnetic effects. • Magnetic forces of attraction and repulsion.	• Energy as a property of many substances and its association with heat, light, electricity, mechanical motion, sound, atomic, nuclei, and the nature of a chemical. • Emission of energy in most chemical and nuclear reactions.	• Constancy of total energy of the universe. • Kinetic and potential energy. • Increase of disorder over time.
		INTERACTIONS OF ENERGY AND MATTER
		• Waves. • Electromagnetic waves. • Wavelengths as substance identifiers. • Conductors, insulators, semiconductors, superconductors.

The chart shows a progression:

- from exploring and describing objects and their movements and orientations in grades K through 4
- to the properties of matter and the motion of objects in grades 5 through 8
- and finally, to the more sophisticated consideration of indirectly perceived structures (e.g. atomic) and relationships in grades 9 through 12.

Before middle grades, a student's experience with objects, motion, and energy centers on exploring one thing at a time. In middle grades, students are able to understand relationships and can graph one measurement in relation to another, such as distance vs force, force vs angle, and intensity or change over time. Graphs are analyzed in the search for possible trends. As they understand ratios and proportions better, students are able to project beyond the data.

Understanding energy, distinguishing between different kinds of energy, and learning about the nature of energy and energy transfer will show a steady progression through this grade level. This section will reflect an appreciation for the specific physical science concepts provided in lower grades, such as understanding the effect of gravity in making things roll, fall, swing, and flow downhill. It shows the kinds of learning that will take place in grades 5 through 8 in physical science, such as testing variables that affect the motion of a pendulum.

Then it looks forward to how students will be prepared to address 9 through 12 grade level concepts and problems that involve determining rates of acceleration of falling or swinging bodies.

PHOTODISC

PHOTODISC

Light On The Wall

The students in my class were engaged in an optical relay race using mirrors to reflect the light from flashlights onto target areas on the classroom wall. Each team of four students had been given a flashlight and a mirror with a distinctive shape. Numbered papers and targets had been taped to the wall.

The room lights were turned off to enhance the effect of the light beams. As the targets were called out, the students took turns spotlighting them with the reflected beams. Student judges kept score. Shining light into people's eyes or onto one another was forbidden. Discussions about winning strategies emphasized the principle of the reflection of light in which the angle of incidence equals the angle of reflection. The activity was connected to a discussion on emergency signaling, the placement of safety mirrors, and other applications.

After the event, one student noted that although the mirror reflected a bright patch of light onto the shaded wall, he could still see the wall even though no direct light shone on it. If we cannot see an object unless light is traveling from that object to our eyes, how did light reach the wall if it was not reflected from our mirrors? This provided a good opportunity to talk about atmospheric scattering of light and about the not-so-obvious reflection of light in our surroundings.

Students were challenged to find and explain a variety of examples of reflected light. For those who needed greater direction, questions were posed, for example:

- Where does glare come from, and how do players in sports keep glare out of their eyes?
- How does clothing next to your face affect your appearance?
- What differences are there between home lighting and industrial lighting?
- How do artists draw shadows to make objects look three dimensional?
- What are the techniques used by photographers to create visual atmospheres?
- How does an interior designer use his expertise about light to create moods? How does a skylight work and what different designs are available?

Students apply the physics of reflection in a game format.

Safety rules must be agreed on before the event.

Concrete experiences should include multiple applications of principles.

Student questions can provide natural transitions within a teaching unit and often give rise to teaching opportunities.

The degree of choice must be adjusted to meet individual student readiness to choose.

- How do shadows change in intensity from morning to night?
- How do clouds reflect city lights at night?
- Which safety devices use reflected light?
- How do we know that particles in the air reflect light?

Individuals or pairs of students used various sources of information, such as printed matter, interviews, light probes, visits to commercial displays, and they use a dollhouse to try out ideas about lighting.

A computer simulation of illumination in an office environment helped students understand the effects of indirect lighting systems. The student groups reported the results of the various investigations to the whole class. The information fell into categories that related to sports, interior design, fashion, visual arts, theater, and safety.

Pat Stonefield, *7th grade science teacher*

New technology extends information resources and exploration platforms.

Content is derived from student effort. Evaluating their reports can assess student effort.

The group chosen was based on the topics resulting from the investigations rather than on topics that had been selected ahead of time.

MAX-KARL WINKLER

PROPERTIES AND CHANGES OF PROPERTIES IN MATTER

Substances have characteristic properties, such as density, boiling points, and solubility, all of which are independent of the size of the sample. A mixture of substances can often be broken down into the original components, or elements, showing one or more of its characteristic properties (NSES, page 154).

Compared to upper elementary level students, middle level students have a better understanding of complex relationships, for example, they are able to understand that:
• density as a ratio of mass to volume.
• boiling point is affected by atmospheric pressure.
• solubility is dependent on pressure and temperature.

An understanding of these relationships is developed by concrete activities that involve hands-on manipulation of apparatus, making quantitative measurements, and interpreting data using graphs.

It is important to connect these characteristics to common experiences so that concepts can be reconstructed as needed, rather than being dependent on rote memory. Some relevant questions are
• What happens in a pressure cooker?

• Why does adding oil to boiling rice and pasta keep it from boiling over?
• What is in antifreeze and how does it keep your carburetor from freezing?

Substances react chemically with other substances to form compounds with different properties. In chemical reactions, the total mass of the reactants is conserved. Substances that react in similar ways are grouped together, as in the case of metals. Students should gain an understanding of rates of change and how different conditions and different substances alter the rates of change.

There are more than 100 known elements. They are able to combine in many ways to produce compounds that make up the living and nonliving substances on Earth (NSES, page 154).

It is easy for students to learn the chemical symbols of the common elements and those that make up common substances. Being able to decipher chemical names on product packages, such as hypochlorite (in bleach) or carbohydrate, calcium carbonate, and trisodium phosphate (in breakfast cereal) is empowering and provides a connection between chemistry and everyday life.

The concept of atoms as the units of matter helps students understand the conservation of matter in chemical reactions.

Carbon is the basic element for living organisms. At this level, students are interested in an introduction to organic chemistry.

A class period describing how chemists work in different specialties introduces the students to careers in chemistry, reinforcing the idea that chemistry is a valuable human endeavor.

MOTIONS AND FORCES

The motion of an object is described by its position, direction of movement, and its speed, and can be represented on a graph. Allow students to interpret graphs that show positive, negative, and irregular relationships. Vector diagrams can be used to differentiate between speed and velocity (velocity has a directional component, speed does not). A variety of instruments for measuring motion include time-lapse photography and strobe lights that "stop" motion.

An object that is not being subjected to a force will continue to move at a constant speed and in a straight line. Although difficult to demonstrate on Earth, with the constant presence of the planet's gravity and the effects of friction, the principle of inertia helps to explain many well-known events like sports action, household accidents, and space walks.

KAREN REYNOLDS

Consider a skater who does not control a turn and continues in a straight line until stopped by a barrier, or an object on a slippery tray that stays behind as the tray moves forward and crashes to the floor.

Perhaps the most difficult part of accounting for the motion or lack of motion of an object is identifying the forces acting on that object compared to the effect of inertia. For example, when a ball is thrown, a forward force is exerted only until the ball leaves the hand after which inertia accounts for the continued forward motion, and gravity accounts for the downward path toward Earth. In The Three Egg High Dive (*Science Scope*, Reynolds Rap), all forces are balanced in the set up and nothing moves until an additional force removes the structures that support

the eggs, which plunge into the cups of water beneath.

If more than one force acts on an object moving along a straight line, the forces will either reinforce each other or cancel each other out, depending on their direction and magnitude. Unbalanced forces will cause changes in the speed or direction of an object's motion. The idea that an object that does not appear to be moving is being acted on by a set of balanced forces is not always easy to grasp because there is no obvious motion involved. Understanding phenomena, such as the sudden collapse of a structure due to unbalanced forces, is often an "Aha!" experience. When students identify forces acting from different directions, they appreciate how moving objects are controlled, and how they overcome friction.

The forces acting on natural and human made structures can be analyzed using computer simulations, physical models, and games like pool, soccer, bowling, and marbles that help to demon-

strate the principles of motion and the effects of collisions. The curved paths of satellites can be explained with the knowledge embedded in this standard.

This is a good place to discuss the connections to traffic safety.

TRANSFER OF ENERGY

Energy, in the form of heat, light, electricity, mechanical motion, sound, and nuclear energy, is a property associated with most substances. Energy is transferred in many ways.

Heat energy involves molecular motion.

Chemical energy depends on the arrangement of atoms and molecules. Mechanical energy is produced by moving bodies or by elasticity.

Potential gravitational energy results from the separation of mutually attracting masses.

Although students have already explored the properties of different kinds of energy, at the middle level students are able to quantify influences on energy transfer and identify multiple step transference within systems. A radio, for example, uses electricity to activate a magnet that produces vibrations that generate sound. Electricity is involved in many energy transfers and provides a fast method of distributing energy to distant locations.

Challenges that involve controlling the amount of energy, or the effects of energy transfer, allow students to describe more complex cause-and-effect relationships. This is an appropriate time to introduce the idea that energy cannot be created or destroyed, only changed from one form into another. Analyzing products or constructing devices from kits can provide engaging learning experiences. Students enjoy historical connections that trace technical applications of knowledge about energy. Addressing issues in local contexts, such as noise pollution, effects of artificial light, and the use of energy resources are also appropriate.

Heat moves in predictable ways, flowing from a warmer object to a cooler one, until both reach the same temperature. The use of instruments to make objective measurements of heat is important. It is interesting to measure heat through sensors in the skin, but it can be misleading. Touching objects that have different heat conduction properties in the same ambient temperature can leave the impression that one object is cooler than the other, when, in fact, one object is carrying heat away from the fingers at a faster rate. Controlling the rate of heat movement, either through direct contact or at a distance, is a technical challenge. Examples in the manufacturing of clothing and machinery abound. Students enjoy contests that involve trying to keep an object cold or warm for a prolonged period. They also enjoy problems that involve analyzing the heat flow properties of different materials and finding out whether they are insulators or conductors.

Matter transmits, refracts, absorbs, scatters, and reflects light. In order for us to see an object, light emitted or scattered from that object must enter our eyes. Explorations with optics should include standard apparatus, such as mirrors, prisms, lenses, and various reflective surfaces. Practical applications of the optical properties of materials are found in cameras, jewelry, safety devises, and televisions. Light waves can be controlled and traced in many ways. Laser beams are used to read bar codes on grocery items and encoded information on compact discs. Special instruments and equipment can extend the sense of sight by detecting and recording light. For example, a telescope focuses light from distant stars, a videocamera records motion that can be seen repeatedly or replayed at different speeds, and infrared and ultraviolet sensors indicate the existence of light outside the visible spectrum.

In most chemical and nuclear reactions, energy is transferred from one system to another. Heat, light, mechanical motion, or electricity might all be involved in such transfers. Most chemical reactions are not explosive, but rather are subtle and hardly noticeable. The transfer of energy associated with many reactions can be detected by monitoring temperature changes. When energy leaves one system, it is transferred into another system. Finding examples from physical, Earth, and life sciences, provide opportunities for exploring and building an understanding of the heat transfer concept. Food chains, food webs, and life cycles are examples of constant energy transfers, that depend on the sun, the ultimate source of energy for life on Earth. Convection cells in the mantle, oceans, and the atmosphere are driven by changes in relative buoyancy resulting from heat absorption and release.

An automobile converts chemical energy (liquid gasoline changes to vapor and is ignited) into heat that produces motion. Energy created by molecular motion in water is released when water vapor condenses or liquid water freezes. Energy in the form of heat is absorbed when ice melts or liquid water evaporates. Finding out how a refrigerator works is a good way to see how heat flow is related to maintaining cool temperatures. The cooling effect of evaporation can be felt when wearing a wet tee shirt or standing under a misting device. As one system gains energy, another system loses energy until a state of equilibrium is established.

RESOURCES FOR THE ROAD

Abell, Sandra K., Anderson, Maria, Ruth, Deb, and **Sattler, Nancy.** (1996, September). What's the Matter? Studying the Concept of Matter in Middle School. *Science Scope, 20* (1), 18–21.

Beichner, Robert J. (1990, May). Paper Cup Magnetism. *Science Scope, 13,* (8), 18–19.

Fowler, Marilyn. (1990, September). Glurch Meets Oobleck. *Science Scope, 14* (1), 21–23.

Hajda, Joey, and Hajda, Lisa B. (1994, November/December). Sparking Interest in Electricity. *Science Scope, 18* (3), 36–39.

Hartman, Dean. (1992, September). Electric Mystery Boxes. *Science Scope, 16* (7), 26–28.

Janulaw, Al. (1993, November/December). The Magnetic Pendulum. *Science Scope, 17* (3), 50–52.

Jones, Richard. (1995, October). How Big, How Tall? The Scaling Principle Answers. *Science Scope, 19* (2), 22–26.

Ostlund, Karen L., and **DiSpezio, Michael A.** (1996, February). Static Electricity Dynamically Explored. *Science Scope, 19* (5), 12–16.

Papacosta, Pan. (1991, May). Electromagnet Dragnet. *Science Scope, 14* (8), 18–21.

Park, John C. (1992, April). Copter Gun Explorations. *Science Scope, 15* (7), 24–26.

Reynolds, Karen. (1983–1997). Reynolds Rap. *Science Scope.*

Sterling, Donna. (1996, October). Discovering Mendeleev's Model. *Science Scope, 20* (2), 26–30.

NIKON #5—Drop of water on reflective material (10x)

Comparison of K–12 NSES Content Standard C: Life Science

The complete text for the Standard related to Physical Science is found in NSES. Each part of the Standard discussed below is identified by its highlighted main statement.

LEVELS K–4	LEVELS 5–8	LEVELS 9–12

CHARACTERISTICS OF ORGANISMS

• Structures of plants and animals and their functions.

• Basic needs of organisms (emphasis on plants and animals). Different environments that support different organisms.

• Behaviors of individual organisms as influenced by internal and external cues. Humans senses.

LIFE CYCLES OF ORGANISMS
• Plants and animal life cycles.

• Parent/offspring resemblance.
• Inherited characteristics and acquired characteristics.

ORGANISMS AND ENVIRONMENTS
• Plant eaters and meat eaters.
• Patterns of behavior in organisms.

• Effects of environmental change.
• Human interaction with and effects on the environment.

STRUCTURE AND FUNCTION IN LIVING SYSTEMS

• Cells as the fundamental unit of life.
• Levels of organization in living systems for structure and function, e.g., cells, organs, tissues, organ systems, whole organisms, and ecosystems.
• Life functions in cells.
• Specialized cells, tissues, and organs and their functions.

• Systems of the human body.
• Diseases and their causes.

REPRODUCTION AND HEREDITY
• Reproduction as essential to a species.
• Sexual reproduction in plants and animals
• Introduction to heredity.
• Genes, chromosomes, inherited human traits.
• Characteristics of an organism resulting from inheritance and from interactions with the environment.

REGULATION AND BEHAVIOR
• Internal conditions for survival.
• Regulation of an organism's internal environment.
• Behavioral responses to stimuli.
• Adaptive behaviors.

POPULATIONS AND ECOSYSTEMS
• Makeup of a population and an ecosystem.
• Producers, consumers, decomposers, food webs.

• Sunlight as the major source of energy
• Limiting factors of biotic and abiotic resources. Population growth and decline.

DIVERSITY AND ADAPTATIONS OF ORGANISMS
• Similarity and diversity in living species.
• Biological diversity and adaptation.

• Species extinction, fossil evidence, rate of extinction.

THE CELL

• Structures underlying cell functions.
• Chemical reactions involved in cell functions.

• DNA.
• Regulation of cell activity.
• Plant cells.

• Multicellular organisms of differentiated cells.

MOLECULAR BASIS OF HEREDITY
• Reproduction is a characteristic of all living systems.

• DNA.
• Chromosomes.
• Mutations.

BEHAVIOR OF ORGANISMS
• Nervous systems in multicellular animals.
• Behavioral responses to stimuli.

• Adaptive logic of behaviors.
• Implications for humans.

INTERDEPENDENCE OF ORGANISMS
• Cycling of atoms and molecules in living and non-living things.
• Energy flow through ecosystems.
• Effects of finite environments and resource on the size of populations.Human modifications of ecosystems.

MATTER, ENERGY, AND ORGANIZATION OF ORGANISMS
• Complexity, and organization of matter, and the processing of energy.
• Food, energy, and adenosine triphosphate (ATP).
• Conservation of matter and energy as they flow through living systems.
• Energy for life.
• Limitations on living systems related to the availability of energy and matter and recycling.
• Tendency towards disorganized states.

BIOLOGICAL EVOLUTION
• Diversity of organisms.
• Interactions that drive evolution.
• Natural selection.
• Descent from common ancestors.
• Biological classifications.

Life Science

As students progress in their development through the grade levels, their focus shifts from the general to the specific and from the simple to the complex. The NSES Standards for Life Science support this transition.

At the elementary level the primary focus is on organisms. Students study the structures, behaviors, and basic needs of organisms while investigating their life cycles and role in the environment.

At the middle level, interest shifts to the cell as the unit of study. Although middle level students continue to observe the behavior and adaptations of organisms, they begin to look at these and at function and reproduction from the point of view of the cell's role as a basic unit of life.

In high school, these same processes are explained at the molecular level. High school students investigate chemical reactions, DNA, and energy transfer as processes that are necessary for life.

The life sciences are a natural topic for middle level students. They are aware of their own developing bodies, and they have a natural concern for other living organisms and our relationship with them. Students are beginning to develop a level of moral concern which permits them to appreciate the role of humans in the environment. They are also interested in their own developing sexuality. The Life Science classroom is an ideal place to provide students with the scientific information they will need to make wise decisions about healthy lifestyles and social behavior.

PHOTODISC

Lively Life Science

I like to engage my students' attention by putting them in the role of real scientists. Once I introduced a lesson by telling them that they would act as animal behavioralists by observing how an animal reacts to changes in its environment. Some of the students had researched the life of Jane Goodall when we did a unit on famous scientists, so they already knew what kind of work an animal behavioralist does.

Suddenly, without warning, I shouted, "HEY!"

I could see the surprise on my students' faces. "How did you react when I yelled at you?"

"Scared." "I wondered what I had done wrong." "I jumped."

"Can you think of some other times when you have had to react suddenly to something around you?"

I followed this demonstration by introducing the concepts of stimulus and response. I asked the students to generate their own definitions based upon their prior experience, but knew that these definitions might change as they carried out their investigations.

The excitement level in the class grew as I introduced the organisms that they were to study. Working in their collaborative groups, the students selected one organism from the collection of crickets, mealworms, crayfish, earthworms, snails, and guppies.

First the groups established a suitable habitat for their organisms. They spent time observing the behavior of their organism and recording their observations.

Next, the students worked together to generate a question that they wanted to answer about their animal. Questions included:

• Will snails respond to chemical stimuli such as salt, vinegar, and ammonia?

Makes connections with literature and uses real-life examples of careers and practicing scientists as role models.

Developing concepts by connecting them to previous experience.

Students are encouraged to work in collaborative groups.

Students develop a baseline of normal behaviors to use as a comparison when stimuli are introduced.

- How do earthworms react to light?
- Do mealworms travel along the edges of a container or do they travel out in the open?
- Are crayfish territorial?
- Do male crickets behave differently around females compared with the way they behave around other males?
- Can guppies learn when to anticipate a feeding?

The groups of students planned their own investigations, then carried out their observations for a few minutes each day over the next few weeks.

> Students should have the opportunity to carry out long-term investigations as well as short activities.

At the end of the observations, the class held a Behavioral Science Convention. Each group was responsible for developing a poster to illustrate their question and their findings. During the convention, each group had time to present what they had found to the class and the class had the opportunity to ask questions about their procedure and findings.

> Students communicate their findings publicly and use peer evaluation as part of their assessment.

Mary Cassini, *6th-grade science teacher*

MAX-KARL WINKLER

PHOTODISC

Structure and Function in Living Systems

Living systems at all levels of organization demonstrate the complementary nature of structure and function. Important levels of organization for structure and function include cells, organs, tissues, organ systems, whole organisms, and ecosystems. (NSES, page 156).

Compared to elementary students who study the structure, function, and needs of plants and animals as organisms, middle level students begin to recognize that cells are the building blocks of organisms and that plant and animal cells differ. They discover that living organisms may consist of one or more cells. All the functions that sustain life act within a single cell. In a multicellular organism, cells specialize, and the work is divided up. Cells are organized into organs such as the brain, stomach, and heart. Different organs are organized into systems such as the nervous system, the digestive system, and the circulatory system. Together, all these

systems make up an organism. Finally, organisms and non-living components make up ecosystems. Specialized structures perform specific functions at all levels of organization.

It is useful for middle level students to think of life being organized in levels, from simple to complex. A high level, such as an organ system, includes everything in the levels below it. A common misconception among middle school students is that each level is independent of the level that precedes it. Using a device such as Russian nesting dolls allows students to visualize the inclusiveness of these hierarchies. Emphasize to students that understanding a lower level, such as single cells, can help explain what is happening at the next higher level.

An analogous system is a car; one must know something about cylinders, spark plugs, and fuel injection and how they interact in order to understand how a car works. In other words, to understand the whole, we need to know about the parts that make it up. Understanding the structure and function of a nerve cell allows us to understand how impulses are transmitted in a branching network of nerve tissue. By knowing the structure and function of a muscle cell, we can understand how muscles work and how they produce movement in an organism.

Understanding how parts relate to the whole also explains certain diseases such as cancer and AIDS, which begin at the cellular level. Other levels of organization that students can relate to include classification systems (kingdom, phylum, class, order, family, genus, species), chemical structure (subatomic particles, atoms, molecules, compounds), structure of the universe (planets, solar systems, galaxies, clusters of galaxies, universe), and ecological systems (organisms, populations, communities, ecosystems).

Teachers can help their middle level students understand this organization of life with activities such as:
• using videodisc clips, microscope slides, photos, and illustrations to compare and contrast different types of cells, describing their shapes, relative sizes, and observable structures.
• comparing individual cells to pictures or slides of tissues and recognize the similarity of cells and how they work together to perform specific functions.
• comparing and contrasting the levels of organization in both plants and animals.
• having students develop their own analogies of parts contributing to the whole (for example, parts and systems of a bicycle).

All organisms are composed of cells—the fundamental unit of life. Most organisms are single cells; other organisms, including humans, are multicellular (NSES, page 156).

All forms of life are composed of cells, from a single-celled paramecium to a multicellular elephant. The cell is the most basic unit capable of performing functions necessary for life. Microscopic, single-celled organisms comprise the greatest biomass of life on Earth, yet students do not recognize the variety and ubiquity of these lifeforms. These single-celled organisms include bacteria, algae, certain fungi, and protozoa.

As single cells, these organisms have special structures that allow them to perform specific functions. Some of these functions are vital to ecosystems and the health of our planet, such as the role of phytoplankton in the carbon dioxide and oxygen cycle. When students see multicellular organisms like elephants and trees, they are actually looking at vast conglomerates of cells. Masses of single-celled organisms can be seen in a tablespoon of bread yeast or in algae mats in a wetland.

It is common for students to think these single-celled organisms are "primitive" compared with familiar large organisms. Emphasize to students that single-celled organisms have many of the same functions as multicellular organisms, such as movement, reproduction, responding to stimuli, acquiring and expending energy, and eliminating waste. They also have similar needs. Certain structures in single-celled organisms perform similar functions in multicellular organisms.

Teachers can reinforce this understanding of the cellular nature of life with activities such as:
• having live cultures available so that students can use a microscope to observe various types of single-celled organisms. This will enable them to understand life at the single-cell level.
• having students collect pond water, then make observations and record them in a journal using diagrams. They should describe the characteristics of various microscopic single-celled organisms, including their movement, behavior, and responses to stimuli.
• using resources on the Internet to observe and describe electron micrographs of single cells and single-celled organisms.
• having students create models of single cells or single-celled organisms using a creative variety of materials. They explain the function of their cell model and how its shape helps it to perform its function.

Cells carry on the many functions needed to sustain life. They grow and divide, thereby producing more cells. This requires that they take in nutrients, which they use to provide energy for the work that cells do and to make the materials

Life Science

that a cell or an organism needs (NSES, page 156).

An organism grows and maintains itself by dividing to form new cells. In multicellular organisms, old cells are constantly dying and being replaced by new cells. To carry out this process, cells must be able to convert and use energy. Some plant cells have special structures to capture energy from sunlight and convert carbon dioxide and water into sugars, a source of energy. Animal cells take in nutrients from their environment to use as energy. Energy is essential to sustaining life.

Many middle school students do not realize that the cell is the basic unit in which life processes occur. They tend to think of cells as the "stuff" that makes up living organisms. Most students understand that the cell is the basic unit of structure in all living matter, but do not think of cells as the basic units of function. Structure and function of cells should be emphasized together, not separately.

It is not easy for middle level students to understand chemical processes that occur at the molecular level in cells, so it is best to avoid developing an understanding of these processes. Instead, students can observe single-celled organisms and maintain cultures of these organisms over time to learn that cells carry out life processes. Starting investigations with single cells

BRUCE THOMAS

such as eggs allows students to observe cells in the process of growing and dividing as evidenced by the changes in an organism's size over time. Single-celled organisms, such as yeast and paramecia, can often be observed in the process of cell division.

An understanding of how cells carry out functions necessary for sustaining life leads to a better understanding of why all living organisms need energy. Energy transfer through a food chain explains how the energy a human obtains from eating a tuna fish sandwich can be traced back to phytoplankton. Students learn everyday examples of important chemical reactions such as photosynthesis and respiration.

Teachers can help to develop ideas related to the life function of cells through activities such as:
• experimenting with yeast cells to determine their energy

needs by adding a yeast culture to a test tube, and placing a balloon over the tube, and measuring the change in size of the balloon; change indicates cellular activity such as respiration and cell division. Compare the growth needs of yeast cells mixed in warm sugar water with yeast cells mixed in warm water alone.
• comparing changes over time in two jars of pond water containing microscopic algae—one with fertilizer and the other without fertilizer.
• experimenting with the effects of different amounts of light on plant growth.

Specialized cells perform specialized functions in multicellular organisms. Groups of specialized cells cooperate to form a tissue, such as muscle. Different tissues are in turn grouped together to form larger functional units, called organs. Each type of cell, tissue, and organ has a distinct structure and set of functions that serve the organism as a whole (NSES, page 156).

While cells contain many of the same structures, these vary considerably in their shape and function. The human body has many different types of cells, each specialized to do a particular job. In most organisms, we see this "division of labor" among different types of cells. We also see a division of labor between different types of tissues and organs. Each one has its own special job to do, but they work together as a system, performing their functions to maintain the life of a multi-cellular organism.

While middle school students understand the concept of the cell as the basic unit of life, they tend to think of cells individually "floating around" on their own, not grouped together to form tissue. Showing students pictures and slides of tissues helps to develop the concept of cells working together with a common function. Slides of epithelial tissue and plant tissue show cells that fit together neatly and are distinguishable from each other. Students can take scrapings from the inside of their cheeks to observe individual cheek cells and compare them to the cells they see in slides or pictures of epithelial tissue. Comparing tissues and cells prepared from onion skin with tissues and cells from elodea leaves helps students realize that different cells have different functions and their structures differ to fit their function. Likewise, comparing human blood cells, nerve cells, and muscle tissues leads to the same conclusion.

Middle level students have a keen interest in their own bodies, so it is important for them to observe a variety of human body cells and tissues. After observing human cells and tissues, such as blood, muscle, nerve, bone, and epithelium, they can observe the same cells and tissues in other organisms. Students

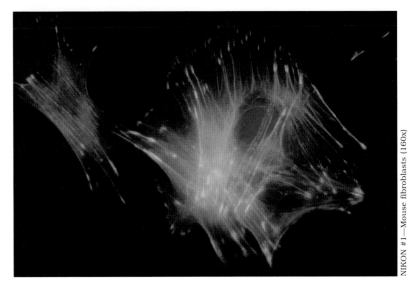

NIKON #1—Mouse fibroblasts (160x)

have prior misconceptions that cells and tissues of different organisms must be very different since the organisms themselves are very different. Comparing and contrasting cells and tissues will allow students to see that the same type of cells and tissues (for example, cardiac muscle) are very similar in many organisms. This leads to developing the concepts of specialized organs and comparing how the same organs have some similar structures and functions in different organisms. It reinforces the concept of unity in life.

The human organism has systems for digestion, respiration, reproduction, circulation, excretion, movement, control, and coordination and for protection from disease. These systems interact with one another. (NSES, pages 156-157).

Organs work together to make up a system. For example, the

digestive system is made up of the esophagus, intestines, stomach, liver, pancreas, and gall bladder. Some organs, like the liver, belong to more than one system. Systems interact with one another. For example, the muscular system, the circulatory system, and the nervous system work together to keep the heart beating.

Middle level is an ideal time to investigate human body systems. (See Standard F, *Science in Personal and Social Perspectives,* for more examples of this topic.) Young adolescents are naturally curious about their bodies and how they function. Instruction should move away from the traditional approach of memorizing the names, organs, and functions of each separate system and move toward investigating the connections between the systems and emphasizing how they function together to maintain an organism.

Students at the middle level need to engage in active exploration to see for themselves how these systems work together. Analyzing data collected by measuring the increase in pulse rate and the rate of respiration with exercise helps students see the connections between the circulatory and respiratory systems. Dissecting chicken wings to see how muscles, tendons, and ligaments work together to make the bones move helps students see connections between the muscular and skeletal systems. In addition, students can discover how the circulatory and nervous systems work together to allow the chicken wing to function.

Disease is a breakdown in structures or functions of an organism. Some diseases are the result of intrinsic failures of the system. Others are the result of damage by infection by other organisms (NSES, page 157).

Microorganisms, such as bac-teria and viruses, can invade the body and cause disease. These are called infectious diseases and can be spread from organism to organism. Non-infectious diseases occur when something goes wrong with the body itself. Part of a system may wear out or stop functioning the way it should. Sometimes these disorders are inherited and other times they are the result of old age, accidents, environmental effects, or unhealthy lifestyles.

Middle school students often feel invincible, so they need to develop healthy lifestyles and an awareness of the causes of disease in order to make healthy lifelong decisions. While some diseases are genetic, students need to understand how personal choices can affect the health of their body systems. For example, choosing to smoke cigarettes can eventually lead to heart and lung disease. Invite speakers from your state Heart Association or Lung Society to give a presentation. These or-ganizations have videos, models, and photos to show the disease effects of smoking.

Exposure to toxic chemicals and radiation can lead eventually to certain forms of cancer and other diseases. Invite speakers from the State Department of Environmental Protection or the American Cancer Society to talk about exposure to environmental hazards. Have your students research the effects of hazardous wastes, oil spills, radon, pesticides and herbicides, ground level ozone, and other environmental agents on human health. Students can interview health professionals, fitness instructors, and nutritionists to learn more about connections between personal health habits and diseases.

Reproduction and Heredity

Reproduction is a characteristic of all living systems; because no individual organism lives forever, reproduction is essential to the continuation of every species. Some organisms reproduce asexually. Other organisms reproduce sexually (NSES, page 157).

Reproduction is one of the basic characteristics of all living organisms. In Standard F, *Science in Personal and Social Perspectives*, the National Science Teachers Association's Position Statement on the Teaching of Human Sexuality is discussed. NSTA contends that "sexuality and the biology of human reproduction [are] essential in the education of every person [and] represent a legitimate component of any teaching program in the life sciences". (*NSTA Handbook, 1997–1998,* Arlington, VA, page 238).

All living organisms have the ability to reproduce. Some reproduce asexually, which means that they do not require a partner. In asexual reproduction, a single organism copies its own genetic material. Some examples of asexual reproduction are fission and budding. Regeneration and vegetative propagation also produce new individuals that are genetically identical to their parent. Sexual reproduction requires two partners, a male and a female, and usually involves the combination of egg and sperm. Unlike other life processes, reproduction is not required for the survival of an individual organism. It is required for the survival of a species since all individuals eventually die.

Using historical examples, such as Francesco Redi's experiment with flies and rotting meat, proves how life arises only from other life. While forms of reproduction vary, the ultimate outcome is that individuals continue to perpetuate their species. At the middle level, students should be observing a variety of organisms and their sexual and asexual methods of reproduction. Culturing bacteria on agar plates demonstrates how, under op-

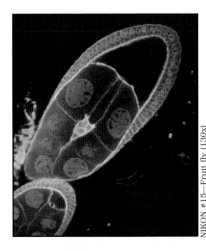

NIKON #15—Fruit fly (130x)

timum conditions, bacteria can multiply quickly through the simple process of fission. Yeast cells can be observed in the process of budding. Cultures of paramecia often show individuals in the process of fission. Be sure to emphasize, however, that single-celled organisms do not reproduce only through asexual means.

Other simple asexual methods to observe in class include hydra budding, regeneration of planaria, and propagating new plants from cuttings. Study sexual reproduction by raising earthworms, insects such as mealworms, guppies, laboratory frogs, and so on. Wisconsin Fast Plants can be used to study sexual reproduction in plants. When students think of egg and sperm in sexual reproduction, they often do not make the connections to the plant kingdom. Pollen is the plant equivalent of sperm, and a plant ovary contains ovules that are fertilized by the pollen.

In many species, including humans, females produce eggs, and males produce sperm. Plants also reproduce sexually—the egg and sperm are produced in the flowers of flowering plants. An egg and sperm unite to begin development of a new individual. That new individual receives genetic information from its mother (via the egg) and its father (via the sperm). Sexually produced offspring are never identical to either of their parents (NSES, page 157).

The making of a new life requires an equal contribution of genes from both the female and male. These genes come from the sex cells. Eggs, produced by females, are round and relatively large. Males produce sperm cells that are about 100 times smaller than the eggs. Fertilization is the process by which a sperm cell fuses with an egg. In sexual reproduction, offspring arise from a new combination of genetic material contributed by both the egg and the sperm. Because of this reshuffling of genetic material, these offspring differ from their parents and from each other, except in the case of identical twins. It is important not to perpetuate the misconception that sexual reproduction results only from a combination of egg and sperm. Simple single-celled organisms like paramecia are able to exchange genetic material without sex cells through a simple process called conjugation.

Tracing the origin of a student's own development back to the sperm and an egg reinforces how life arose from a combination of male and female sex cells. There are some excellent video resources that show the combination of egg and sperm resulting in a zygote and its development. Ask students if they look identical to either of their parents and if they have particular traits that resemble either parent. Discussing similar, but not identical, traits leads to an understanding of how students receive genetic information from both parents and how the new combination results in their unique characteristics. Some students hold the misconception that their traits came from their mother's genes or father's genes but not from a combination of the two. There are several physical models that can be used with students to demonstrate a reshuffling of genetic information derived from both parents. Noting the different characteristics of students shows how sexual reproduction leads to variety in a species.

Every organism requires a set of instructions for specifying its traits. Heredity is the passage of these instructions from one generation to the next (NSES, page 157).

Organisms receive, or inherit, their traits from their parents. Humans will have opposable thumbs whereas dogs will not. Dogs inherit their paw struc-

NIKON #7—Red and green algae (20x)

ture from their parents and humans inherit their hand structure from their parents. Each type of organism has its own particular traits but these can vary from generation to generation. Heredity involves passing on these traits.

Before students are introduced to the genetic explanation of heredity, they should be able to identify traits by observation. Observing similarities and differences between organisms of the same species leads to an understanding of traits and how traits from both parents are passed on to produce new individuals with combinations of traits from both parents. Observable traits such as eye color, ear lobes, height, hair texture, and so forth, can be identified and traced back to their parents and possible grandparents. Great care and sensitivity should be taken, however, since some students' family situations will not provide this information. Teach-

ers can use geneological charts or hypothetical examples to demonstrate the passage of traits.

Hereditary information is contained in genes, located in the chromosomes of each cell. Each gene carries a single unit of information. An inherited trait of an individual can be determined by one or by many genes, and a single gene can influence more than one trait. A human cell contains many thousands of different genes (NSES, page 157).

In the 1860s, Gregor Mendel discovered that there were factors that affected inheritance in pea plants. He had no idea of how these traits were passed on at the cellular level. Later, in the 1890s, chromosomes were discovered and suspected to be the carriers of trait information. In the early 1900s, Mendel's factors were determined to be genes located on chromosomes. We now know that single genes and combinations of genes are responsible for an organism's traits. Different organisms have different numbers of chromosomes and genes resulting in a variety of gene combinations arising from sexual reproduction. Each organism has a gene for a particular trait from each parent. This combination of genes is called the genotype. For example, a particular genotype of a trait might contain a blue-eyed gene and a brown-eyed gene. The actual observable effect of the genotype is called the phenotype—in this case, brown eyes.

Different organisms have genes for different traits. Genes are found on chromosomes. One common misconception among middle level students is that more complex organisms have a greater number of chromosomes. Humans have twenty-three pairs of chromosomes while a potato plant has forty-four. Having students research and graph chromosome numbers will address this misconception.

Genes explain how "hidden traits" emerge in new generations. The question "How come my eyes are blue if both of my parents have brown eyes?" leads to exploring the concepts of dominant and recessive genes, genotypes, and phenotypes. Pink flowers resulting from crossing genes of red and white flowers illustrates concepts like blending. Simple coin tosses show how new gene combinations can result in new combinations of traits.

Investigating different gene crosses through models such as coin tossing and other simulations helps students understand how new gene combinations arise. Be careful not to make it too simplistic; not all genes separate independently, and there can be two forms. Discussion of alleles and codominant alleles should be held at a later grade level. Introduce Punnett squares and simple probability so that students can make

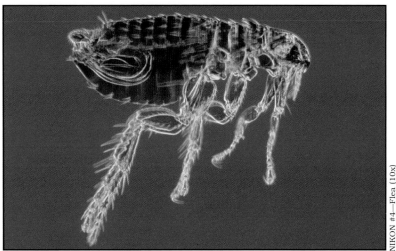

NIKON #4—Flea (10x)

predictions about gene crosses. Commercial seeds, such as albino corn seeds, can be obtained from scientific supply companies and planted to predict genotypes and phenotypes of offspring when the parent genotypes are known. Students should have actual hands-on experiences setting up and analyzing the effects of crossing different genes. Wisconsin Fast Plant seeds can be purchased with different traits that can be crossed and analyzed in class.

The characteristics of an organism can be described in terms of a combination of traits. Some traits are inherited and others result from interactions with the environment (NSES, page 157).

Eye color, skin color, and hair texture are inherited traits. Wearing colored contact lenses, using tanning cremes, and getting a hair permanent do not change the genetic makeup but

can temporarily change the way one looks. Genetic characteristics will be passed on from generation to generation whereas changes induced by interactions with the environment usually will not be passed on. Sometimes interactions between heredity and environment determine particular behaviors in plants and animals. For example, adult monarch butterflies usually live for approximately two weeks, and during this time they reproduce and die. Shorter days and colder temperatures trigger a genetic signal to the last generation of monarchs in the north to migrate to Mexico. They return to the United States in the spring to start a new generation.

Having students investigate a variety of ways appearances can change due to environmental factors can lead to a discussion of genetics versus environment. When students are examining traits in class, often they will iden-

PHOTODISC

though conditions in the environment change. For example, even though the temperature outside may be freezing, humans keep an internal body temperature of approximately 98.6 degrees Fahrenheit.

Because of the variety of living organisms, students believe there must be very different requirements for maintaining life. Students need opportunities to investigate a variety of organisms to realize that their fundamental needs are alike. All organisms are composed of cells and the basic requirements of cells are essentially the same whether they belong to cells of a human, plant, fungi, protist, or bacterium. They all have similar metabolic processes such as digestion, respiration, and excretion. They must adjust internal conditions in response to external factors. Most reproduce to enable a species to survive. It is important to emphasize that while there are similarities, there are also differences. For example, plants and animals obtain energy in different ways. Animals must acquire food in order to produce energy whereas plants are able to utilize energy from the sun to make their own food that they store as energy.

Middle school students often confuse the terms "food" and "energy." Developing an understanding of photosynthesis and respiration helps students to understand the

tify curly hair that has been permed as a trait for curly hair, or brown hair that has been dyed blond as a trait for blond hair. Give them an example of a cat that lost its tail in an accident. Will all its kittens be missing a tail?

Interactions between genetics and the environment lead to interesting discussions. Heart disease is a good example. Some people have a genetic history of heart disease. Others do not, but because of poor lifestyle choices such as smoking and a high fat diet, are predisposed to heart problems. Those with a previous genetic history of heart disease need to be aware of environmental factors that can increase their risk.

Have students discuss other real-life examples such as skill in basketball. Is it inherited or does it come from repeated practice? Do genetic traits such as height and handspan increase basketball

skill? How does "nature versus nurture" play a role?

Regulation And Behavior

All organisms must be able to obtain and use resources, grow, reproduce, and maintain stable internal conditions while living in a constantly changing external environment (NSES, page 157).

There are many different types of living organisms, but they all perform similar tasks to maintain life. All organisms must take in food and gases from their environment to provide energy. Most organisms grow as they progress through their life cycle. Often this growth is accompanied by changes in appearance such as a caterpillar growing and changing into a butterfly. The ability to reproduce ensures species continuation. Homeostasis is the ability of an organism to keep conditions inside the body the same, even

process of energy conversion. Another misconception students have is that all organisms need oxygen to live. Anaerobic organisms, such as different types of bacteria, cannot survive in the presence of oxygen. Students can observe how bacteria respond to different levels of oxygen by creating mud columns and observing growth and response over time.

Organisms grow at different rates and differ in ultimate size. Students sometimes confuse growth in multicellular organisms only with "cells get larger" instead of "cells get larger and more cells are produced." Hormones play a role in the growth process. Students may want to investigate giantism and dwarfism to determine the role hormones play in the growth process. Students may think that plants grow as humans do, proportionally increasing in all their parts and eventually ceasing to grow when they are adult. Observing trees shows how they continue to grow taller throughout their life span, but their branches always seem to be the same distance from the ground. Most trees will continue to grow taller for as long as they live. Plants are ideal organisms to use for studying growth since they respond to a variety of environmental stimuli. Light, gravity, temperature, and the length of night and day are all environmental factors that can be investigated for their effects on plant growth.

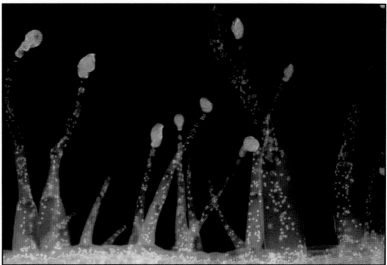

NIKON #12—Tobacco leaf (50x)

During early adolescence, boys' and girls' bodies begin to change. Hormones produced by the reproductive system initiate puberty and mark the beginning of sexual maturity which is a sensitive topic that needs to be addressed.

The principle of homeostasis should be introduced at the middle level. To show the significance of this concept, have students investigate how their bodies stay warm, how they control their blood sugar, and the amount of water in their bodies. A common misunderstanding is that all these conditions are controlled exclusively by the brain (nervous system). As students discover how systems of the body work together, they will understand the various control mechanisms that regulate these systems, including the endocrine system.

Regulation of an organism's internal environment involves sensing the internal environ- *ment and changing physiological activities to keep conditions within the range required to survive* (NSES, page 157).

Stability is essential to every organism's survival. The endocrine system helps maintain internal stability by secreting hormones into the bloodstream to regulate the life processes. For example, after a meal, insulin is released to promote the storage of excess blood sugar as glycogen. Without maintaining a relatively stable internal environment, life processes would cease, and an organism would perish.

Many students believe that the body is controlled exclusively by the nervous system. This is an ideal time to show how systems work together, such as the nervous and endocrine system that controls our internal environment. Use real-life experiences such as the time you were frightened and could feel your heartbeat increase due to the increase in adrenaline. This demonstrates how the release of hormones causes changes in your body. This sudden change supplies quick energy for a rapid response.

This is a good time to compare and contrast how messages are sent through the body. The nervous system uses nerve impulses to send messages, whereas the endocrine system uses chemicals (hormones).

To understand how the endocrine system works, use the analogy of a feedback mechanism. A refrigerator has a thermostat that controls the temperature of the refrigerator so food will not freeze nor become too warm. If the door is open for too long, the thermostat senses a change in the internal temperature and makes the motor work harder to remove heat from inside the refrigerator. When the temperature is stable, the motor does not have to work as hard and conditions inside the refrigerator remain stable.

Behavior is one kind of response an organism can make to an internal or environmental stimulus. A behavioral response requires coordination and communication at many levels, including cells, organ systems, and whole organisms. Behavioral response is a set of actions determined in part by heredity and in part from experience (NSES, page 157).

Behavioral responses help organisms to adjust to a variety of environments. Like internal regulatory actions, behavioral responses are triggered by either external or internal stimuli. Once the stimulus is detected, the event is communicated to other cells. The increased number of cells involved produces a coordinated response that affects the organism's actions. Behavior can be innate or learned. Innate behaviors are passed on to offspring genetically from their parents. For example, an Atlantic salmon knows instinctively to return to freshwater to lay its eggs, and newborn mammals do not need to be taught how to nurse. Learned behavior is not inherited and results from experiences after birth such as learning to tie your shoes or to spell.

Animals have evolved a variety of behaviors to help them respond to changes in the internal or external environment. Students may have difficulty distinguishing between behaviors that are learned and behaviors that are passed on through heredity. Give students an opportunity to think about their own behavior, or the behavior of animals with which they are familiar, to help them distinguish between learned and inherited behaviors.

Ethologists study animal behavior. Students can become amateur ethologists and go to a zoo or other area where they can develop data collection skills as they make observations of learned and instinctive animal behavior. As students investigate the nervous system, they can make connections between the nervous system and other body systems, showing how a coordinated effort between systems produces a response. It is important for students to realize that the nervous system does not operate in isolation—it works with all the other body systems to control reactions and behaviors.

An organism's behavior evolves through adaptation to its environment. How a species moves, obtains food, reproduces, and responds to danger are based in the species' evolutionary history (NSES, page 157).

Organisms have characteristics and behaviors that enhance their chances for survival. These characteristics and behaviors are called adaptations. Many adaptations have arisen through natural selection. During environmental change, offspring inherit their surviving parents' successful adaptations and pass them on to the next generation.

A common misconception among middle school students is that organisms are able to effect an immediate change in their body structure or change their normal behavior in response to a change in their environment. These changes do not happen immediately. Adaptations happen over long periods of time and are passed on by successful offspring to new generations. Investigating live organisms or observing organisms on video reveals several adaptations that have occurred over time to enable an organism to survive in its environment.

Populations And Ecosystems

KAREN REYNOLDS

A population consists of all individuals of a species that occur together at a given time and place. All populations living together and the physical factors with which they interact compose an ecosystem (NSES, page 157).

Ecosystems can be large like a tropical rain forest or small like a crack in a sidewalk. They can be terrestrial or aquatic. A tide pool is an example of an ecosystem. There are several different populations in the tidepool. Periwinkles, rockweed, and barnacles are examples of different populations. Each population is affected by conditions such as the salinity of the water, temperature, and dissolved oxygen.

Middle school students understand populations and ecosystems best when they have an opportunity to explore them actively. Taking students to a pond, a tidepool, or a field, or even having them observe life under a rotting log, allows them to identify

and observe interactions between populations and identify the physical conditions needed for their survival. Ecosystems are often confused with habitats. Habitats can be described as a population's "address" in an ecosystem. For example, lily pads can be found along the edges of lakes where the water is not too deep. The edge of the lake is their habitat but the entire lake is their ecosystem.

Middle school students think of ecosystems as vast areas of land or water and often confuse them with biomes. Ecosystems can be large, like a Northern Maine forest, or as small as a pond. A classroom aquarium, terrarium, or river tank can serve as an excellent model for observing ecosystems and the changes and interactions that occur over time between populations of organisms and physical conditions. Videos and videodiscs provide visual opportunities to explore a variety of ecosystems and

populations of organisms.

Populations of organisms can be categorized by the function they serve in an ecosystem. Plants and some microorganisms are producers—they make their own food. All animals, including humans, are consumers, which obtain food by eating other organisms. Decomposers, primarily bacteria and fungi, are consumers that use waste materials and dead organisms for food. Food webs identify the relationships among producers, consumers, and decomposers in an ecosystem (NSES, pages 157–158).

In a pond food web, many different food chains connect to form a branching network of feeding relationships. The producers and consumers can be eaten by more than one kind of organism. The plants and microscopic algae in the pond are the producers. They are able to capture energy from sunlight to make their own food. Organisms such as snails, zooplankton, insects, and small fish feed on the plants and algae. These organisms are called the primary consumers. In turn, other animals feed on the primary consumers. For example, larger fish, turtles, or frogs might feed on the insects. These are called secondary consumers. Tertiary consumers feed on the secondary consumers and might also feed on the primary consumers. For example, the frogs might be eaten by the snapping turtle which might also eat small fish. The top consumers in the food web usually are not eaten by other animals, but are broken down eventually by the decomposers when they die.

During the elementary school years, students concentrated on linear food chains. Food webs are non-linear and branch out in several directions. Initially diagrams of food webs can be initially confusing to middle level students. When students are guided to construct their own webs and make links between organisms, the relationships become clear. Creating a bulletin board with pictures of organisms in a particular ecosystem and letting students use yarn to make the connections reinforces the concepts of different organisms eating the same food. Food chains show linearly how one organism is eaten by another. Food webs show multiple relationships. Students assume that the higher the level in a chain, the larger the

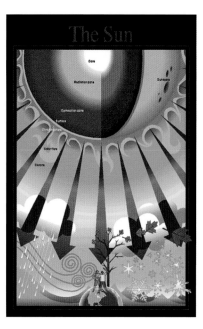

organism will be. Using examples such as a shrew (for a secondary consumer) and an elephant (primary consumer) clearly show that size is not related to an organism's role in a food chain or web.

For ecosystems, the major source of energy is sunlight. Energy entering ecosystems as sunlight is transferred by producers into chemical energy by photosynthesis. That energy then passes from organism to organism in food webs (NSES, page 158).

All food can be traced back to sunlight. The energy stored in plants by photosynthesis is passed on from an organism at one level to organisms at higher levels in the food web. An energy pyramid is used to show visually how energy is lost as it moves up through the levels from producers to consumers. The greatest amount of energy

is stored in the producers. Some energy is lost at each level of the food web as organisms use up energy for their life processes. An organism at the top of the food web has the least amount of stored energy.

All living organisms need energy to live and grow. Eventually all energy from food can be traced back to the sun. Ask students to describe a scenario in which the sun suddenly disappears. Students learn that Earth will grow cold and dark, but plants will no longer grow, and animals that feed on the plants will die. The animals that feed on the animals that ate the plants will also die. Students should learn to distinguish the differences between the way plants and animals obtain food and how the energy they need to sustain life comes from what they eat. Food is the fuel and building material for all organisms, yet not all substances taken in by organisms are considered food in the biological sense. Plants also take in water and minerals, but it is the sugars and starches that are considered "food." Students need to understand that food is transformed into energy, and that certain foods, like carbohydrates, are high in energy.

The number of organisms an ecosystem can support depends on the resources available and abiotic factors, such as quantity of light and water, range of temperatures, and soil composition. Given adequate biotic and abiotic re-

sources and no disease or predators, populations (including human) increase at rapid rates. Lack of resources and other factors, such as predation and climate, limit the growth of populations in specific niches in the ecosystem (NSES, page 158).

Biotic resources include all the living components of an ecosystem such as bacteria, fungi, plants, and animals. The abiotic resources include the non-living parts. The interactions between the biotic and abiotic resources comprise the ecosystem. For example, certain plants require acidic soil and trout require oxygen-rich water. Some organisms respond to abiotic factors, such as changes in temperature, by growing heavy winter coats, burrowing deep into the mud, or migrating south in the winter. An organism that cannot adapt to changing abiotic conditions may not survive. A niche is the specific role that an organism occupies in an ecosystem. Each organism has its own niche. If two organisms occupy the same niche, there will be competition and the population of one or both organisms will decrease. Climate and predation help control populations. Mosquito populations in ponds decrease as cold weather arrives. Predators, such as dragonflies and bats, keep mosquito populations in check.

Increases in population are difficult to understand without a visual model. Hav-

ing students graph an exponential growth graph shows how quickly populations can increase if there are no external controls. Plants grown in the classroom can be used to observe the effects of limited resources such as light, food, and space. A common misconception is that a niche relates to an organism's role. Students often think of niches in terms of where an organism lives. The concept needs to include what an organism eats, how it gets water, where it lives, and what it needs to be able to reproduce. Examining local ecosystems and

NIKON #HM4—Crustacean. (30x)

discovering niches occupied by different organisms helps develop this understanding. While a variety of print and video resources can be used, allow middle level students to investigate actual ecosystems whenever possible.

Diversity And Adaptations Of Organisms

Millions of species of animals, plants, and microorganisms are alive today. Although different species might look dissimilar, the unity among organisms becomes apparent

from an analysis of internal structures, the similarity of their chemical processes, and the evidence of common ancestry (NSES, page 158).

Animals and plants vary in body plans and internal structures. The similarities in internal structures help biologists infer the degree of relatedness among organisms. Even developmental characteristics, particularly at the early embryo stage, show similarities. Similar types of cells, tissues, and organs are observed in a variety of species, and similar chemical processes such as photosynthesis and respiration occur in a variety of organisms across the five kingdoms. All organisms convert and use energy.

Evidence of a common ancestry can be inferred from fossil evidence and the similarity of DNA. Modern classification is based on evolutionary relationships that suggest similarities even among the diversity of living organisms. Groups or organisms share characteristics that came from a common ancestor. These characteristics are used for classifying organisms into groups. Within each group are other groups that are distinguished by their own unique characteristics. Examining these unique characteristics helps us discover evolutionary patterns.

In the middle grades, students should have many opportunities to enrich their growing knowledge of biological diversity. Teachers of social studies and science can combine the study of geography with biological diversity. Similarities between organisms in different parts of the world, such as tigers and mountain lions, show evidence of common ancestors. As students investigate different types of organisms, guide them toward thinking about their similarities and differences.

Have students construct their own classification systems and compare them to the systems used by biologists to classify organisms and the reasons those characteristics are used. Students learn that classification is not arbitrary and that it is used to make sense of the diversity and interconnectedness of organisms. They begin to understand hierarchical relationships as they progress from kingdom level to species. Middle level is a good time to investigate single-celled organisms from simple bacteria to more complex protists. Students can see similarities in the structure they use for movement. Students begin to wonder about viruses and their relationship to living things.

A common misconception in the early grades is not understanding what an "animal" is. Students often confuse animals with vertebrates. This is a good time to investigate a variety of animals including sponges, worms, mollusks, and so on. Examining fossil histories shows how simple organisms appeared first and how more complex species evolved later. Homology can be introduced at the middle level to show similarities in structure. Using diagrams that show the bone structure in fish fins, whale flippers, bird wings, frog legs, and human arms indicates similar forelimbs and allows students to infer that these organisms must have had a common ancestor.

Biological evolution accounts for the diversity of species developed through gradual processes over many generations. Species acquire many of their unique characteristics through biological adaptation, which involved the selection of naturally occurring variations in populations. Biological adaptations include changes in structures, behaviors, or physiology that enhance survival and reproductive success in a particular environment (NSES, page 158).

A characteristic, structure, or behavior that helps an organism survive in its environment is called an adaptation. Adaptations help organisms get food, protect themselves, move, reproduce, and carry out their life processes. Organisms that adapt best to their environment survive to pass their traits on to their offspring. This process, discovered by Charles Darwin, is called "natural selection." It explains how a species can change over time and also how new species arise when they are isolated from other members of their species such as on an island or separated by land or water. Members of the isolated population adapt to changing conditions and often pass new and different traits on to their offspring. As a result, new species arise that may look and behave totally different from the original. The pouched marsupials of Australia and animals of the Galapagos are good examples.

One of the misconceptions middle level students have is that these adaptations do not occur by chance. Some students believe that organisms adapt to environmental changes intentionally by modifying their structures, behavior, or physiology. Students do not see change as a random process that affects only a few individuals in a population. They think of all individuals responding to change that happens quickly rather than over a long time period. Design your instruction specifically to prevent or uncover these misconceptions since students tend to adhere strongly to their own misunderstandings. Using examples such as Darwin's finches or the peppered moths of Manchester helps students develop an understanding of natural selection over time.

Extinction of a species occurs when the environment changes and the adaptive characteristics of a species are insufficient to allow its survival. Fossils indicate that many organisms that lived long ago are extinct.

Life Science

Extinction of species is common; most of the species that have lived on the earth no long exist (NSES, page 158).

Fossils show that many organisms that lived in the past were different from organisms living today. Fossils record evidence of life forms that once existed far back in time and show that many organisms in the past became extinct. More than 99 percent of all organisms that ever lived are now extinct.

Middle level students often believe that extinction is caused by humans and is therefore unnatural. If students have opportunities to examine the fossil record, they will conclude that extinction is a natural process that has affected most of Earth's species over time. Few organisms that were alive during early geologic time exist today. Providing students with fossil evidence and allowing them time to construct their own explanations is important in developing middle level understanding. Students should have opportunities to hypothesize about the effects of environmental change and catastrophic events on organisms and populations.

RESOURCES FOR THE ROAD

Bollwinkel, Carl W. (1990, November/December). Keeping Pace with Snails. *Science Scope, 14* (3), 30–32.

Budd, Kathryn S. (1997, March). Critters for a Day. *Science Scope, 20* (6), 42–43.

Dungey, Joan M. (1997, March). Growing Our Own Outdoor Science Lab. *Science Scope, 20* (6), 74–76.

Grambo, Gregory. (1995, May). Raising Butterflies in Your Classroom. *Science Scope, 18* (8), 16–18.

Harrell, Pamela Esprívalo. (1997, January). Dragon Genetics. *Science Scope, 20* (4), 33–37.

Ma, Peggy R. (1993, October). On Golden Pond. *Science Scope, 17* (2), 10–13.

Shriver, Marti, Teresa David, and Charlene Stewart. (1997, March). Research—Mud, Bugs & Fun. *Science Scope, 20* (6), 46–49.

NIKON #3—HeLa cells (300x)

Comparison of K–12 NSES Content Standard D: Earth and Space Science

The complete text for the Standard related to Earth and Space Science is found in NSES. Each part of the Standard discussed below is identified by its highlighted main statement.

LEVELS K–4	LEVELS 5–8	LEVELS 9–12
PROPERTIES OF EARTH MATERIALS • Earth materials, their physical and chemical properties, and use as resources. • Properties of soils. • Fossils as evidence.	**STRUCTURE OF THE EARTH SYSTEM** • Layers of the solid Earth. • Lithospheric plate movement. • Land forms resulting from constructive and destructive forces.	**ENERGY IN THE EARTH SYSTEM** • Internal and external energy sources. • Convection in the mantle and plate movement. • Convection within the atmosphere and oceans. • Global climate.
OBJECTS IN THE SKY • Describing objects in the sky (The sun, moon, stars, clouds, birds, and other things). • Light and heat from the sun.	**EARTH'S HISTORY** • Comparing past and present Earth processes. • Effects of occasional catastrophic events. • Fossil evidence of changes in life and environments.	**ORIGIN AND EVOLUTION OF THE EARTH SYSTEM** • Origin of the solar system and planet Earth. • Rock and fossil evidence to estimate geologic time. • Ongoing processes of evolution within the Earth system. • Early evidence of life.
CHANGES IN EARTH AND SKY • Slow and rapid changes on the surface of the Earth. • Daily and seasonal weather changes. Measurement of temperature, wind direction and speed, precipitation, and other quantities. • Daily and seasonal patterns of movement of sun and moon. Cyclic change of the moon's shape.	**EARTH IN THE SOLAR SYSTEM** • The solar system. • Effect of gravity on motions within the solar system, holding objects to the surface of Earth, and on tides. • Motions that explain such phenomena as the day, the year, phases of the moon, and eclipses. • The sun as the major source of energy for phenomena on Earth's surface, such as growth of plants, winds, ocean currents, and the water cycle. Causes of seasons.	**ORIGIN AND EVOLUTION OF THE UNIVERSE** • Theory of origin of the universe. • Formation of visible mass in the universe. • Energy and element production in stars. **GEOCHEMICAL CYCLES** • Geochemical cycles of Earth elements. • Movement of matter between chemical reservoirs.

Earth and Space Science

Earth science provides a rich and varied curriculum because it includes many distinct fields of science, such as meteorology, astronomy, geology, paleontology, and biology, as well as the many specialties within these fields. In addition, it integrates principles of physics, chemistry, and mathematics, and biology. Students in the elementary Earth sciences learn to observe objects and natural features, and the motion of planets and stars. In contrast, middle level students focus on explaining these observations. Many Earth science phenomena are only understood through indirect evidence and involve changes that occur slowly. We do not see mountains rise, and Earth's progress around the sun is not readily apparent.

Middle level students begin to understand time in terms of millions of years and learn that Earth and astronomic processes have a long history. They are able to grasp that events such as erosion and mountain building or evaporation and precipitation occur at the same time. Because Earth processes cannot be repeated on command nor observed in convenient locations for short periods of time, we rely on models and comparisons between the present and past to help students understand Earth science concepts. Learning about dynamic forces and cause-and-effect relationships provides a foundation for high school-level coverage of geologic and astronomic evolution, geochemical cycles, and advanced concepts related to energy in the Earth system.

Many ideas in Earth science are developed by professionals and accepted as the truth by students. Students should be given opportunities to explore for themselves how to gather evidence about events that cannot be seen directly and to gain a deeper understanding of the principles and concepts that explain the history and the phenomena of Earth's systems. Much instruction in Earth science involves helping students to make concrete connections between the principles of general science and the specific contexts of Earth science.

PHOTODISC

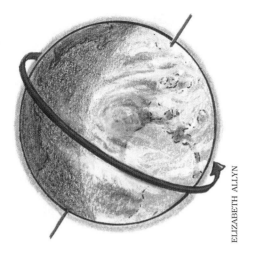

ELIZABETH ALLYN

All Day ... All Night

(For a supporting picture, capture a Web site photo from a 24-hour videocam, of Mt. Fuji, a beach, or other feature— better yet, capture several for a sort of collage or mosaic of contrasting photos—this was done by NSTA staff members for a recent Reynolds Rap column on 24-hour videocams.)

Sometime during the fall students asked me how the times for sunrise and sunset could be printed in the newspaper so far in advance. After I explained the power of making accurate predictions from well established patterns, the students discussed how they had always believed what they were told about Earth's rotation and that the side of the Earth that is in shadow experiences night while the side facing the sun is in daylight. Except for photographs of Earth from space, they had never seen it for themselves.They then accepted the challenge of checking out the day/night phenomenon on the Internet using 24-hour video-cameras, which served as extensions of their eyes, and allowed them to see live pictures of many locations on the Earth's surface simultaneously.

After searching the Internet for videocams and 24-hour cams, I located Tommy's List of Worldwide Cams at http://chili.rt66.com/ozone/cam.htm as a good starting point for the students. Since searching on the Internet could become an all-consuming task, students were limited to 10 minute sessions and were required to state their objectives before beginning. The students soon found that team work was beneficial and began linking their objectives so as to increase their progress and follow interesting leads.

The inquiry began with mapping and verifying night and day over the globe, which I extended to mapping and verifying weather conditions. At first I was concerned that students would use their Internet privileges for off-task activities. I found that providing key prompts related to the current topic, hands-on lab activities, assignments with Internet search options, and asking students to give

Opportunities for inquiry often come from student questions and discussion.

Teachers should check out the Internet and provide some guidelines before making Internet access too open ended

Validating students' efforts is an effective monitoring device. Connecting student-driven use of resources to concrete class activities facilitates student-centered construction of knowledge and expands understanding in different contexts

10 second updates at the beginning of the class, kept most efforts within the curriculum. After a few weeks, students began grouping areas of interest and teams were allowed to specialize or spend more time monitoring specific sites. Popular themes were Antarctica, beaches, volcanoes, a variety of countries, and certain cities. These locations were monitored for temperature, weather, atmospheric visibility, and other data.

Students kept journals on their explorations and findings and often saved images to their personal disks for including in multimedia presentations. I read their journals frequently and helped individuals and teams formulate additional questions and lines of inquiry. The use of the Internet for Earth science explorations became a yearlong endeavor and engaged many students' time outside of class. Connections with geography, mathematics, and other subject areas were pointed out frequently by the students themselves.

Manuel Rodriguez, *8th grade science teacher*

Journals provide ongoing individualized assessment of the acquisition of knowledge, processing information, and developing reporting abilities

Becoming aware of connections between science and other content, and learning to learn are important goals for scientific literacy.

MAX-KARL WINKLER

Structure of the Earth System

The solid Earth is layered with a lithosphere, a hot, convecting mantle, and dense, metallic core (NSES, page 159).

What is a system? It is an assemblage of parts forming a unitary whole. Change in one segment of the whole will tend to affect every other segment.

Earth has four main systems: the atmosphere, the hydrosphere, the biosphere, and the geosphere. Within these systems material is constantly being reworked by the great cycles such as the water cycle, the rock cycle, and the carbon cycle. Physical forces, chemical reactions, heat, energy, and biological processes all interact with each other and with Earth's great systems.

To understand the geosphere and the rock cycle students begin by learning about the relationship between the upper part of the lithosphere, which is called the crust, and the layers of rock that underlie it. They should investigate buoyancy using several materials so that they recognize the effects of the differences in density of the phases of matter namely, gases, liquids, and solids. For example, a brick falls through the air because it is denser than air. Marshmallows float on chocolate milk. Hot air rises through cooler, denser air. Continents float on the denser mantle. Movement of material in the Earth's mantle can be demonstrated by the classic model of a convection cell in a tank of water into which students pour colored cold water and colored warm water in order to see the dynamics of convection.

We cannot reach the mantle and Earth's core, but geologists are able to map them and determine their composition and movement using indirect evidence, models, and experimenting with similar materials. For example, if we listen to sounds traveling through air, wood, metal, and water, we detect differences that allow us to interpret the nature of the sound carrier. Instruments are used to make sonic profiles of petroleum bearing structures and rock formations beneath Earth's surface. Earthquake waves provide information about the crust itself and the deep layers beneath the crust.

Earth's magnetic field is generated by its rotating metallic core. Concepts of density differences, movement due to convection, and moving magnetic fields can be connected to physics, meteorology, cooking, technological developments and human history, and many other areas of study.

Plates of lithosphere on the size of continents and oceans move constantly at a rate of centimeters per year in response movements in the mantle.

Major geological events, such as earthquakes, volcanic eruptions, and mountain building, result from these plate motions (NSES, page 160).

Several types of sound waves generated by earthquakes are received at different times at seismic recording stations around the world, allowing geophysicists to pinpoint the epicenters of earthquakes. Mapping these epicenters and the sites of volcanic activity reveals the boundaries between plates of lithosphere. Although only those large earthquakes that damage areas inhabited by humans are featured in the news, earthquakes occur every day world wide. Students can access data on the Internet on the occurrence of earthquakes.

Mountain building, such as in the Alps in Europe and the Himalayas in Asia, is caused by plates ramming into each other. The Andes evolved, and are still evolving, as a result of a subduction zone pushing an oceanic plate eastward under the South American continent. The Hawaiian island chain is the result of an oceanic plate in the Pacific Ocean moving across a "hot spot" in the mantle which causes the overlying rock to melt and erupt as volcanoes. This builds islands and mountains from the ocean floor to heights well above sea level. Animations of

Earth's movements since the time of the supercontinent Pangaea help students see the global dynamics. They can be challenged to produce their own animations or claymation videos or multimedia demonstrations of plate movements.

Land forms are the result of a combination of constructive and destructive forces. Constructive forces include crustal deformation, volcanic eruptions, and deposition of sediment, while destructive forces include weathering and erosion (NSES, page160).

Although these forces and the resulting mountain building, valley formation, and evolution of other land features are easy to understand as isolated processes, students may have trouble visualizing the effects because both constructive and destructive forces operate at the same time. In order to understand land forms it is important for students to learn to interpret cross sections and to produce their own pictorial renditions of erosional and tectonic sequences. Computers can be useful here. Visualizing geologic processes needs three dimensional thinking and recognition of the long periods of time involved. Some processes that occur on land also occur beneath the ocean but they will produce different results because the physical characteristics of water are quite different to the characteristics of air and water. Students should observe weathering to

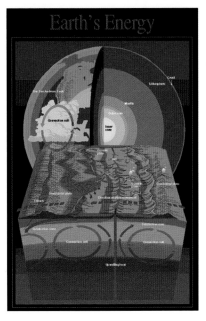

learn about the constancy of this process and they should visit local examples of our attempts to control erosion and weathering. Examples include sidewalks, street gutters, paint and varnish on outside structures, drainage ditches, dams, terracing, channeled streambeds, levees on river banks, seawalls, and breakwaters. Preventing damage requires knowing what caused the damage. Students can be challenged to design a solution to an authentic erosion problem in the community.

High-and low-level aerial photographs and space images reveal phenomena on Earth's surface that can be identified and studied. Some of these are geologic and geographic features, the seasons of the year, the time of day, the direction of water flow or prevailing winds, topographic

relief, variation in rocks and soil, the distance that material suspended in water will travel in an ocean or a lake, vegetation, and areas of human habitation. Sources of photographs range from citizens' views from high places (scenic overlooks, high buildings, out airplane windows) to government agencies such as the National Aeronautics and Space Administration (NASA), United States Geological Survey (USGS), National Oceanic and Atmospheric Administration (NOAA), and Bureau of Land Management (BLM).

Connections to human history can be interesting. Besides catastrophic events, such as volcanic eruptions, earthquakes and floods, geographic barriers have challenged humans and channeled their activities and movements in many interesting ways. Students might consider how history might have been different if the Nile flowed south instead of north, if the North American continent were not joined to the South American continent, or if the Mississippi valley were 100 meters lower.

Earth's History

The Earth processes we see today, including erosion, the movement of lithospheric plates, and changes in atmospheric composition, are similar to those that occurred in the past (NSES, page160).

Earth's history has been punctuated by occasional

catastrophic events, such as the impact of an asteroid or a comet, enormous volcanic eruptions, periods of continental glaciation, and the rise and fall of sea level.

Although El Niño is a media event during certain years, it is a natural phenomenon that has affected atmospheric conditions periodically over the centuries.

We learn about changes in Earth's past from the evidence in:

- sedimentary rocks such as limestone, sandstone, phosphates and shale
- volcanic flows, flood deposits, and beach sands
- glacial deposits that tell of past ice ages and global cooling and warming
- fossil beds that enable us to match rocks from different continents
- fossil beds that show how organisms developed though very long periods of time.

The periodic changes in the magnetic orientation of metallic minerals in iron-bearing rocks give evidence of reversals in Earth's magnetic field. Craters manifest the impact of meteors or larger bodies such as asteroids or comets.

Scientists predict the possible effects of Earth processes so as to provide information for making decisions related to human safety. An understanding of Earth's systems leads to a fuller use of natural resources. Scientific literacy distinguishes between scientific information that relates to a societal decision, and the decision-making process itself. Students may

PHOTODISC

engage in debates on social studies related to rerouting river water, depleting ground water supplies, building structures on soils that are suitable for growing crops, damming rivers, beach control and replacement, and other issues in which social interests interact with geologic processes. Human development can be affected by whether we can or cannot change Earth processes.

Fossils

Fossils provide important evidence of how life and environmental conditions have changed (NSES, page 160).

Fossils provide information about the development of life, the extinction of species, the ages of geologic formations, plate tectonics, the history of Earth, the distribution of organisms, climatic cycles and other changes. One of the first states to require that oceanography be part of the science curriculum was Nebraska, which has rich deposits of ancient marine fossils. Fossils occur in all parts of the country, and by collecting local specimens students can connect them to the geologic history of their area. Museums provide collections to which amateurs and professionals can compare their samples. Finding fossilized shark teeth is not uncommon at sites where old marine sediments have eroded and become part of modern beaches. Students finding seashell fossils on a mountain top can puzzle over whether they indicate uplift or very high ancient sea levels. Some sedimentary rocks may have many different kinds of fossils, allowing students to find out which organisms lived at the same time. Students investigate certain organisms whose shells coil in one direction during warm periods and the other direction during cold periods. It takes the accurate identification of many fossils to produce useful composite bodies of information. Not all paleontologists hunt for Tyrannosaurus Rex. Many fossils are small, even microscopic. Fossils are our most important source of information about life on Earth in the distant past. Some fossils produce economic gains, for instance diatomaceous earths which are composed of silica, are used in toothpaste and other cleaning abrasives. Our fossil fuels were originally plants and animals. Learning to recognize fossils and knowing how to learn more about them can provide enjoyment for a life-time.

Earth in the Solar System

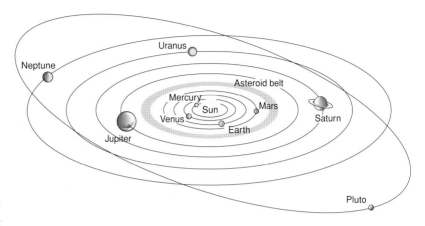

The earth is the third planet from the sun in a system that includes the moon, the sun, eight other planets and their moons, and smaller objects, such as asteroids and comets. The sun, an average star, is the central and largest body in the solar system (NSES, page 160).

The similarities and differences between the objects in the solar system are fascinating in themselves. Energy radiates from the sun and travels outward falling on all bodies in the solar system at strengths inversely proportional to their distances from the sun. With appropriate filters, and the assistance of experienced astronomers, students can view the sun-spots and the solar storms that project into space. There are numerous resources on the Internet for downloading images of the sun, planets, comets, asteroids, and other bodies. NASA and other organizations maintain Web sites for teachers, students, and the public for posting updates on current missions. Surfing the Internet to look for information on the solar system is something that parents and

students can do at home. There are programs that interested individuals can use to ask questions of professionals, and to contribute their own observations and discoveries to the knowledge base.

Most objects in the solar system are in regular and predictable motion. Those motions explain such phenomena as the day, the year, phases of the moon, and eclipses (NSES, page 160).

Understanding how the motion of objects in the solar system are tracked, measured, analyzed, and predicted involves:

- developing abilities in spatial relationships
- using instruments and models
- making mathematical calculations.

Hands-on models and computer-based simulations are helpful for understanding relative motion and seeing the solar system from different perspectives.

Students can find out about the Explorer, Voyager, and Galileo missions, other space probes and even design their own. The motion of the moon and certain planets can be observed by tracking their positions and phases during one or more months. Students should be allowed to calculate the motion for themselves by watching demonstrations, manipulating objects, drawing diagrams, creating computer-based animations, and explaining their results to others in their own words. They should use tide tables to investigate the relationship between the phases of the moon and changes in sea level.

Students should learn to appreciate the power of prediction that lies in mathematics when it is based on careful quantitative observations. As an extension, students should research the long history of observing the movement of objects in the sky described by humans from many cultures over thousands of years. Expert sky watchers have been pivotal in making decisions for migrations, planting, navigating, worshipping, and carrying out other human activities.

Gravity is the force that keeps planets in orbit around the sun and governs the rest of the motion in the solar system (NSES, page 161).

Gravity alone holds us onto the surface of the Earth. When students are asked how conditions on a space shuttle differ from conditions here on Earth, they often respond with "no gravity" rather than the better answer which is that "the effects of gravity are not felt." Experiments related to microgravity can be carried out on space shuttles and in orbiting space stations because the effect of the Earth's gravitational pull has been "neutralized." By comparing how much a person would weigh on each planet, and knowing that the differences in weight are due to differences in gravity, students can begin to distinguish between mass and weight.

Understanding the effects of gravitational forces helps explain the ocean tides. Seeing the Earth-Moon relationship as a kind of majorette's baton, twirling with its own center of gravity, gives interesting insights. By orbiting

satellites and space probes around planets, scientists have taken advantage of the planetary fields of gravity to increase the acceleration of the space craft. In this way scientists are able to "sling" the craft into paths calculated to reach distant parts of the solar system.

Investigating the forces acting on objects on Earth, accounting for the part gravity plays leads students to an understanding of the balance of forces, equilibrium, structural support systems, friction, trajectories, buoyancy, and other science concepts.

The sun is the major source of energy for phenomena on the earth's surface such as the growth of plants, winds, ocean currents, and the water cycle (NSES, page 161).

The tilt of the Earth's axis (23.5 degrees) accounts for the change of seasons and the length of days, by causing variations in the amount of the sun's energy that hits Earth's surface. To understand that the sun is a major source of energy for phenomena, students might trace energy chains to the ultimate source (always the sun) in such things as the food they eat, patterns of motion in the atmosphere and hydrosphere, cloud formation and other parts of the water cycle, and the formation of petroleum

and other fuels. To correct misconceptions such as "seasons depend on the distance between the Earth and the sun," requires considering clusters of concepts. Understanding the cause of seasons involves understanding that light energy from the sun arrives in parallel rays that :

• are less concentrated when they impact a surface at a low angle to rather than at the perpendicular

• provide an amount of energy to a location in direct relation to the amount of time of exposure

• vary from one latitude to another due to the tilt of the Earth's axis

• shift during the year as the Earth's tilt exposes different hemispheres to them as the planet journeys around the sun.

It is the collective effect of all of these ideas that makes understanding the cause of seasons more appropriate for middle grades than for primary grades where teaching the subject is often attempted.

The role of the Sun in causing seasons and global wind patterns can be illustrated by considering what would happen if:

• Earth rotated once a year with the same side always facing the sun

• Earth rotated once a month

• Earth's axis were not tilted

• a combination of any of the previous conditions.

Banks, Dale A. (1994, January). Earth, Sun, and Moon: A Moving Experience. *Science Scope, 17* (4), 36–41.

Brendzel, Sharon. (1994, April). Schoolyard Erosion and Terrain Studies. *Science Scope, 17* (7), 36–38.

Bull, Linda. (1995, November/December). Ceiling to Floor Astronomy. *Science Scope, 19* (3), 19–21.

Cronin, Jim. (1996, November/December). Teaching Astronomy with Multicultural Mythology. *Science Scope, 19* (3), 15–17.

Emery, Dave. (1996, October). A Constructivist Cloud Lab. *Science Scope, 20* (2), 18–19.

Koons, Bill. (1997, May). Map and Compass Lab. *Science Scope, 20* (8), 22–24.

Langdon, Robert J. (1995, September). Dig Into Mining Activities. *Science Scope, 19* (1), 28–33.

Lebofsky, Nancy R., and **Lebofsky, Larry A.** (1996, November/December). Celestial Storytelling. *Science Scope, 19* (3), 18–21.

Matthews, Catherine, Fargo, Dick, and **Craig, Jeffrey.** (1997, January). Build an Interplanetary Scale. *Science Scope, 19* (4), 24–26.

Seagar, Douglas B. (1993, November/December). Where in the World? *Science Scope, 17* (3), 14–18.

Weigel, Shannon. (1996, February). The Earth and the Sun: A Seasonal Misconception. *Science Scope, 19* (5), 30–33.

Woods, Robin K. (1996, October). Simulating Glaciers: Stimulating Interest in Geology. *Science Scope, 19* (2), 10–13.

Wright, Rita F. (1993, January). How High Is Your House? *Science Scope, 16* (4), 16–19.

NIKON #HM1—Alkali-gabbro crystal. Polarized light (2x)

Comparison of K–12 NSES Content Standard E: Science and Technlolgy

The complete text for the Standard related to Science and Technology Science is found in NSES. Each part of the Standard discussed below is identified by its highlighted main statement.

LEVELS K–4	LEVELS 5–8	LEVELS 9–12
ABILITIES OF TECHNOLOGICAL DESIGN	**ABILITIES OF TECHNOLOGICAL DESIGN**	**ABILITIES OF TECHNOLOGICAL DESIGN**
• Identify a simple problem.	• Identify appropriate problems for technological design.	• Identify a problem or design an opportunity.
• Propose a solution.	• Design a solution or product.	• Propose designs and choose between alternative solutions.
• Implementing proposed solutions.	• Implement a proposed design.	• Implement a proposed solution.
• Evaluate a product or design.	• Evaluate completed technological designs or products.	• Evaluate the solution and its consequences.
• Communicate a problem, design, and solution.	• Communicate the process of technological design.	• Communicate the problem, process, and solution.
UNDERSTANDING ABOUT SCIENCE AND TECHNOLOGY	**UNDERSTANDINGS ABOUT SCIENCE AND TECHNOLOGY**	**UNDERSTANDING ABOUT SCIENCE AND TECHNOLOGY**
• Science's role in answering questions and explaining the natural world.	• Comparing scientific inquiry and technological design. Comparing the work of scientists to that of engineers. Benefits and consequences of technological solutions.	• Differences among disciplines. Interdisciplinary teamwork. Emergence of new discipline.
• Scientists and engineers working in teams.		
• Contributions of women and men of all ages, backgrounds, and groups.	• Contributions to science and technology by many people and cultures.	
• Tools and techniques for solving problems; predicting effects to avoid further problems.	• Ways in which science and technology are reciprocal.	• Reciprocity of advances in science and technology.
• Tools that help scientists make better observations, measurements, and equipment for investigations.		• Need for creativity, imagination, and good knowledge base.
	• Limitations and tradeoffs in technological solutions.	
	• Improving safety and reducing risks.	
	• Constraints in technological designs.	
	• Intended and unintended benefits of technological solutions. Predictable and unpredictable consequences.	• Comparison of purposes and nature of scientific inquiry and technological design.
		• Public access to scientific and technical knowledge.
ABILITIES TO DISTINGUISH BETWEEN NATURAL OBJECTS AND OBJECTS MADE BY HUMANS		
• Identifying natural and designed objects.		

Science and Technology

The Standard focuses on the skills that students should develop in order to produce effective designs for a new technology as well as developing the knowledge and attitudes necessary to appreciate the role that science and technology play in our society.

A clear progression is evident in the Standard:

- from simple design applications that do not distinguish between science and technology in grades K through 4
- to the identification and design of applications that are distinctly technological in application in grades 5 through 8
- and finally, to the design of a technological solution to a problem and the evaluation of the consequences of that solution.

Before the middle grades, students are aware that technology has given us products that make our lives better. However, these students often do not have the historical context to understand what life was like before the technology was available. They rarely distinguish between applied science and technologic applications.

Middle level students are beginning to have enough life experience to see some technological revolutions occurring during their young lives. For example, they can appreciate the advances in computer technology because, just in the last few years, they have seen computers use more global connections and become faster and smaller.

Middle level students now begin to distinguish between science and technology. They understand that technology focuses primarily on solving human needs or on creating new products. Science is the foundation of technology, and new technologies (such as the scanning electron microscope) have been necessary prerequisites for breakthroughs in science.

There is also a progression in the understanding of science and technology. Young children recognize that scientists and engineers, from all backgrounds, work together to develop new products and ideas to help society. By the middle level grades, the students begin to differentiate between the kind of work performed by scientists and by engineers. They also begin to appreciate that technology is not the magic answer to all problems and that sometimes there are negative as well as positive implications to new technologies.

PHOTODISC

Puzzling Over Science

I have always enjoyed puzzles, so it is probably no surprise that I love to teach with puzzles. One of my favorite techniques is to use Rube Goldberg designs. He was the cartoonist who drew fantastic machines for solving problems. One day, as my students entered the room, I had a large poster based on a Rube Goldberg idea hanging in the front of the room. The students were interested. Several of them came up to the front for a closer look before taking their seats.

"Does anybody have any idea what this is?" I asked.

"It looks like a maze." "It's funny." "Do you think it would work?"

I explained that this was inspired by a man named Rube Goldberg. He created complex and amusing devices for solving simple problems. We walked through the sequences and talked about how each one would work and what the end result would be. Questions included:

- What is the function of this part of the machine?
- Can you design a different part that would do the same thing?
- What changes will make this machine work faster? In reverse?

Then it was time for the students to go to work. We divided into cooperative groups, and I gave them the assignment to create blueprints for devices that would wake them up in the morning (I knew that a lot of my students had trouble getting out of bed in the morning and could relate to this challenge).

The students went right to work. As I went around the class looking at their creations, I reminded them to be sure that each part of the device was based upon a physical principle.

During the next period each group had a chance to present its device to the class. The students walked through their designs and pointed out the different physical principles that they were using.

When all the student groups had finished, we talked about some examples of ways in which technology had improved society. I was even able to get some examples of illustrations of patent applications from different periods of history to show the students the kinds of innovations that have changed our society.

John Walters, *6th grade science teacher*

Students are led through the evaluation of the design, considering the strengths and weaknesses of different components.

Scientists and engineers work together in teams to solve design problems.

Student should have practice analyzing their designs.

MAX-KARL WINKLER

Science and Technology

Abilities Of Technological Design

During the middle school years, students should be presented with a variety of experiences that highlight advances in technology. It is best to focus these activities on meeting a human need, solving a problem, or developing a product.

All classroom technology experiences and tasks should be well defined. Students like to solve problems to which they can relate. The tasks should be based upon familiar knowledge that engages only one or two main ideas. Since the emphasis is on design, the construction of devices should not be time consuming or tedious.

This can be achieved by investigating a variety of familiar objects, including simple tools such as: screwdrivers and hammers; levers and pulleys; more complex tools such as hand-held mixers and can openers; and electronic devices like radios, telephones, and microwave ovens. Through the application of critical thinking skills, the students can compare, contrast, and assess these items for cost, practicality, environmental effects, safety, and convenience. Through their investigations, students will come to appreciate the interplay of scientific concepts and social and economic issues.

PHOTODISC

In the middle grades, the five-stage model for technology design, introduced in the elementary Science and Technology Standards, is built on by increasing the complexity of the problems addressed.

• *Identify appropriate problems for technological design.*

Students at the middle level grades begin identifying those human problems that can be addressed by technology. They can be challenged to invent new tools or to consider technological advances that would help society. They should be able to develop criteria for evaluating the product. Who is the audience for the product? How will we know if the product meets their needs?

• *Design a solution or a product.*

Using their own criteria, students design several ways of solving the problem and evaluating the best approach. They should be encouraged to consider the time, cost, benefits, and risks in deciding which design to use.

• *Implement a proposed design.*

Where appropriate, students can actually construct their devices. This might also be a good opportunity to bring in pictures of historic patent models of common devices to demonstrate to the students how inventors go about developing and patenting new devices.

• *Evaluate completed technological designs or products.*

Students should be encouraged to evaluate their designs critically in terms of the criteria that they have developed for this use. They should ask themselves questions like: How would you improve your design? How does your design benefit society? Are there any risks or negative implications to your design? If so, are these risks worth taking given the possible benefits that might come from the device? As an example, you might point out that early microwave ovens carried a risk for patients who used pacemaker devices, but the benefits to society, in general, were considered to outweigh the possible risk to those few who had the heart device.

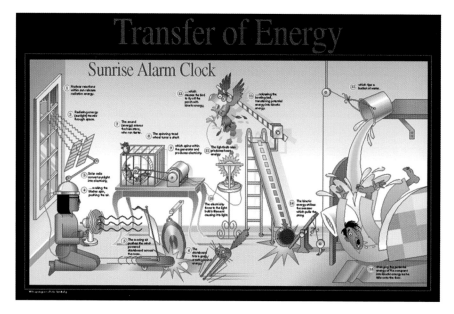

For a more elaborate discussion of this topic, see *Standard G, History and Nature of Science.*

Perfectly designed solutions do not exist. All technologies have trade-offs.....Technological designs have constraints...Technological solutions have intended benefits and unintended consequences. (NSES, page 166)

Middle level students are able to evaluate the impact of technologies, recognizing that most have both positive and negative impacts on society. The critical factors are revealed in the analysis of the benefits and risks. Do the benefits of the technology outweigh the risks to society? They should also begin to recognize that technologies have limitations, not only in terms of what society will accept as a risk, but also in the physical limitations of materials and in the scope of our knowledge. The speed of computers, for example, is limited by:
- the laws of physics stating that electrons can only move at a certain speed
- the available materials
- and by the knowledge of manufacturing currently at our disposal.

There are many ways that teachers can involve their students in design activities. Building a tower out of drink-

- *Communicate the process of technological design.*

Students should keep a log of their designs and evaluations so that they can share developments with others. The log might address questions such as: What is the function of the device that you have designed? How does the device work? How did you come up with the idea for the design? What were the sequential steps you took in constructing your design? What problems did you encounter in the design or construction?

Understanding About Science And Technology

Scientific inquiry and technological design have similarities and differences... Science and technology are reciprocal. Science helps drive technology...

Technology is essential to science (NSES, page 166).

The primary difference between science and technology is that science focuses on answering questions about the natural world and engineering applies scientific principles to the solution of human problems. Middle school students begin to appreciate the differences between these two and to distinguish between scientific advances and technological breakthroughs. Yet the two are closely linked. Technology depends upon the principles and methods of science, just as science has advanced through new instrumentation and approaches emerging from technology and engineering.

Many different people in different cultures have made and continue to make contributions to science and technology (NSES, page 166).

ing straws is a good start for collaborative work, design preparation, and construction. More elaborate projects might include constructing a balloon out of paper or plastic, or mousetrap-powered cars.

The National Science Teachers Association administers a contest open to students in grades 4, 5, and 6 and sponsored by Sears, Roebuck and Co. It is called the *Craftsman/ NSTA Young Inventors Awards Program.* Students are encouraged to combine their creativity and imagination with science, technology, and mechanical ability to invent and build a tool or modify an existing tool. The goals of the program are to teach students to understand the scientific principles underlying tools, to encourage creative thinking, and to allow students to develop practical solutions to everyday problems.

For more information about the program, write to: **Craftsman/NSTA Young Inventors Awards Program,** National Science Teachers Association, 1840 Wilson Boulevard, Arlington, VA 22201-3000

RESOURCES FOR THE ROAD

Berger, Carl F., Lu, Casey R., Belzer, Sharon J., and **Voss, Burton E.** (1994). Research on the Uses of Technology in Science Education, in Gabel, Dorothy L. (ed.), *Handbook of Research on Science Teaching and Learning,* New York: Macmillan Publishing, 466–490.

Cox, Jim. (1994, January). Rube Goldberg Contraptions. *Science Scope, 17* (4), 44–47.

Etchison, Cindy. (1995, April). Tales from a Technology Teacher. *Science and Children, 3* (7), 19–21, 30.

Mechling, Kenneth. (1991, February). Consumer Cohorts. *Science Scope, 14* (5), 20–23.

(1996, March). Technology in the Classroom. (Theme issue) *Science Scope, 19* (6).

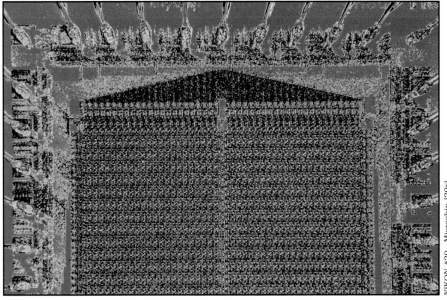

NIKON #20—Microchip (20x)

Comparison of K–12 NSES Content Standard F: Science in Personal and Social Perspectives

The complete text for the Standard related to Science in Personal and Social Perspectives is found in NSES. Each part of the standard discussed below is identified by its highlighted main statement.

LEVELS K–4	LEVELS 5–8	LEVELS 9–12
PERSONAL HEALTH	**PERSONAL HEALTH**	**PERSONAL AND COMMUNITY HEALTH**
• Safety and security as basic needs of humans. • Individual responsibility for own health. Personal care.	• Need for injury prevention. • Importance of regular exercise and physical fitness to the maintenance and improvement of health.	• Responding to hazards and accident potential. • Personal control of fitness.
• Nutrition for health. How the body uses food and how various foods contribute to health. Recommendations for good nutrition. • Substances that can damage the body and how it functions. • Beneficial substances. Inappropriate uses.	• Consequences of variations in nutrition. • Consequences of tobacco use. • Substance abuse including alcohol and other drugs.	• Interaction between nutrition and personal well-being and social factors. • Effects of substances on mood and behavior.
	• Sex drive as a natural human function that requires understanding. Sexually transmitted diseases. • Maintaining environmental health.	• Human sexuality. • Function of families in serving basic health needs. • Severity and control of diseases.
CHARACTERISTICS AND CHANGES IN POPULATIONS	**POPULATIONS, RESOURCES, AND ENVIRONMENTS**	**POPULATION GROWTH**
• Human populations and the number of individuals of a particular population that live in a given amount of space. • How the size of a human population can increase or decrease.	• Effects of overpopulation.	• Dynamics of population growth. • Factors affecting birth rates and fertility rates. • Limitations to population carrying capacity.
TYPES OF RESOURCES		**NATURAL RESOURCES**
• What things are resources. • Basic materials and resources made of basic materials.		• Natural resources that support human populations.
• Limited supplies; recycling and extended use.	• Causes of environmental degradation and resource depletion.	• Interaction between humans and natural systems. • Earth's finite resources.
	NATURAL HAZARDS	**NATURAL AND HUMAN-INDUCED HAZARDS**
	• Natural hazards caused by internal and external processes of the Earth. • Human activities that can induce hazards. • Natural hazards that present personal and societal challenges.	• Normalcy of natural hazards. • Effect of human activity on potential for natural hazards. • Kinds of hazards.

LEVELS K–4	LEVELS 5–8	LEVELS 9–12
	RISKS AND BENEFITS • Risk analysis and use for reducing or eliminating risks. • Risks associated with natural, chemical, biological, social, and personal hazards. • Use of a systematic approach to thinking critically about risks and benefits. • Basing decisions on perceptions of benefits and risks.	• Risk assessment—science and technology in local challenges. • How people continue to invent and innovate, with different effects on others. Predicting how ideas and inventions will affect other people. • Ways that science and technology have improved our lives. These benefits are not worldwide.
	SCIENCE AND TECHNOLOGY IN SOCIETY • Influences of science on society. • Social priorities and research. • Influence of technology on society. • Contributions of science and technology to society. • Variety of settings in which scientists and engineers work. • Ethical codes for research involving humans. • Limitations of science and technology in solving human problems.	**SCIENCE AND TECHNOLOGY IN LOCAL, NATIONAL, AND GLOBAL CHALLENGES** • Role of understanding principles of science and technology in the process of debate. • Interaction between social issues and advances in science and technology. • Human decision-making. • Effects of humans on other species and the environment. • Considering risks and benefits.
CHANGES IN ENVIRONMENTS • What is meant by environments. • Changes in environments and some effects. • Environmental changes that occur slowly, and that occur rapidly and their consequences.		**ENVIRONMENTAL QUALITY** • Interaction between humans and processes of natural ecosystems. • Effects of materials produced by society on physical and chemical cycles of the earth. • Factors affecting environmental quality.

Science in Personal and Social Perspectives

The National Science Education Standards assert that middle level students need opportunities to apply science-based solutions to personal and social issues. But middle level teachers do not need national standards to tell them how important it is to help their students make wise decisions. At a stage in their lives when personal identity and social interactions are most important, early adolescents need opportunities to make science a part of that identity and their daily decision making.

While grappling with personal decisions such as protecting themselves from the sun's ultraviolet radiation, choosing healthful rather than junk food, or choosing to act with sexual responsibility, middle level students are bombarded by media and peer influences that have little to do with the science of these matters.

How young people approach social issues depends upon what they value. If they are given opportunities to observe and appreciate their natural setting, students will be more likely than not to think and act responsibly about environmental issues and natural hazards. School experiences that nurture students' abilities to think and act scientifically and solve problems cooperatively equip them with the thinking tools to resolve complex societal issues that involve applying scientific knowledge. An awareness of their own bodies may encourage students to make healthy choices and wise decisions about their personal safety.

Middle level students hold a variety of misconceptions concerning personal and social issues related to science. Many middle level students

believe that the effects of their actions, decisions, and choices are unrelated to the quality of their health and the protection of the environment. They may regard humans as an indestructible species and consider some resources, such as the oceans, to be limitless. The misconception that technology can be invented to solve any problem limits creative problem solving and undermines the appropriate use of technology.

Although this standard addresses a diversity of topics, it is unified by focusing on the individual's role and responsibilities in the following areas: personal health, populations, resources and environments, natural hazards, risks and benefits, and science and technology in society. Students are called upon to weigh personal benefit against what is good for society.

As middle level students become more autonomous, they will make better personal and social decisions. The middle level teachers' role is to facilitate their independence through science experiences upon which the students can base responsible choices and through which they can live more interesting and productive lives.

PHOTODISC

The Great Fitness Test

I know that my students are keenly aware of their changing bodies. The boys are becoming more involved in athletics and proud of their developing muscles. The girls seem obsessed with how they look (and how others think they look). Given that innate interest, I decided to develop a lesson focused on helping the students to understand their growth and development better.

I decided to set up stations in the room, each addressing a different aspect of physical fitness. Each station had appropriate equipment for the students to use in collecting data. There was a biofeedback monitor, an electronic blood pressure device, a light gate for pulse indication, lung capacity apparatus, digital thermometers, meter sticks for measuring height, a bathroom scale, stethoscopes, and cardiovascular fitness software. I had instructions for the use of each piece of equipment. We also have some computers in the room that allow me to display the data graphically for the students at the end of the experiment.

All was ready for the lesson. As the students came into the room, they were surprised to see so much health-related equipment out on the tables.

"Hey, Ms. Baker. Are we having gym class in here today?"

"No. But we are going to be talking about the science of physical fitness. What do you think it means to be physically fit?"

This led to a lively discussion about exercising, eating correctly, getting enough sleep, and staying away from substances that would cause harm, like drugs and alcohol . As we talked, we realized that physical fitness was a difficult term to define concretely. It was time to move to the laboratory.

I started by dividing the class into teams—each assigned to one of the physical fitness stations. Their task was to learn about their station:
- how the equipment worked
- how to record data

> Focusing on topics that are of interest to students is a great way to increase motivation and help them see the relevance of science in their lives.

> Use of technology to support science instruction.

> Starting the lesson with a reference to the students' prior knowledge allows them to develop conceptual anchors for the new information to be learned.

- describe what measurements the data is recording
- "teach" this to the rest of the class.

Once all of the students understood how to use the equipment, they began collecting data to define physical fitness. I was careful to check before class to see if any of the students had breathing difficulties caused by asthma or other physical conditions. I emphasized that if a student had difficulty with any of the tasks, he or she should let me know immediately. I was also concerned about students being self-conscious about their weight, so I made weighing an optional activity.

It took three lab periods for all of the students to complete each of the stations, but it was time well spent. As I reviewed their lab notes, I could see that the students had created charts for recording their observations and they were gathering the quantitative data that they would need for our discussion.

As we examined the data, we noticed some interesting trends. There were striking differences in fitness levels between the individual students. There were also some trends in the data. For example, the lung capacity of the students who were on the swim team or who played a musical instrument was greater than those who did not.

The students left the lesson with a much better understanding of physical fitness. They learned that they had the ability to control very specific aspects of their own health. As a follow-up activity, each student generated a list of activities that would improve specific aspects of his or her own physical fitness.

Lin Cheng, *8th-grade science teacher*

> Student ownership of learning can be enhanced when they are made responsible for the task and for sharing it with others.

> Importance of a focus on safety while conducting the lab activity.

> Students identify, through their own data collection, a relationship between exercise and lung capacity.

MAX-KARL WINKLER

Personal Health

Regular exercise is important to the maintenance and improvement of health (NSES, page 168).

Food provides energy and nutrients for growth and development (NSES, page 168).

When students accept the idea that their long-term health and well-being is dependent on day-to-day choices, they also accept the task of making everyday decisions. This is difficult for middle level students who are focused on the here and now. They often view themselves as indestructible and certainly have difficulty understanding that decisions they make today may have an impact upon their lives when they are 20 years or older. Standing in the way of students' acceptance of this challenge is the misconception that some outside force (parents, school, the law) is ruling their lives, when the students actually make many daily decisions independent of these forces. It is easy for a middle level student who seems to have his or her whole life ahead to rationalize that it is acceptable to eat a bag of potato chips instead of an apple for a snack, or to choose watching TV instead of playing intramural sports after school.

When parents and teachers work in partnership, they can help the middle level students take on the challenge of

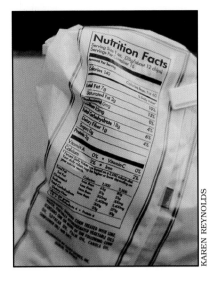

KAREN REYNOLDS

maintaining personal health. Schools can also accept this challenge by eliminating sources of temptation like snack food and soft drink machines and replace these with healthier options.

As students begin to see themselves in charge of their own health, their teachers should help them differentiate between factors over which they have control, such as weight, exercise, and healthy habits, and those factors which they cannot control, such as genetic traits.

Science teachers can reinforce the importance of making healthy decisions by having students:
- measure and record their heart rate during various forms of activity. Graphing and comparing active heart rates with resting heart rates will give an indication of cardiovascular fitness.
- make a personal plan for physical fitness. Compare

these plans with guidelines for physical fitness found on the President's Council for Physical Fitness Web page:
http://www.hoptechno.com/book11.htm.

The potential for accidents and the existence of hazards imposes the need for injury prevention. Safe living involves the development and use of safety precautions and the recognition of risk in personal decision (NSES, page 168).

Middle level students are overwhelmed by social pressures. Sometimes these peer pressures lead the early adolescent to engage in reckless activities. Just being told that it is important to wear a helmet when riding a bike, roller blading, or skateboarding will not overcome the peer attitude that helmets are not a "cool" look when cool is important at the age of thirteen. It will take a clear understanding of the trauma of head injuries in bicycle or skateboarding accidents and investigations of the physics of such injuries to get that helmet on a middle level student's head. This is where science can provide the data. Middle level students will soon be behind the wheel of a car. They are told that wearing a seat belt when riding in or driving a car is important and that it is the law. For some young people, however, being told the right thing to do does not make it happen. Science class investigations of motion and force gives the young driver informa-

BRUCE THOMAS

tion and experiences for assessing risk and making decisions.

Some of the activities that teachers might share with their students include:
- designing a "crash test" for apples (or peaches), comparing those covered with bubble-wrap packaging to fruit without that protective wrap. Let the fruit sit for a day after their "crash," then cut them open to assess the damage.
- researching data on the types of injuries to bicycle riders who had accidents while wearing helmets, compared to those who had accidents and were not wearing helmets. Compare this research to the fruit "crash" data.
- inviting a representative from the State Highway Patrol to demonstrate the "Convincer," a low-speed collision simulator, so students can feel the effects of wearing a

seat belt during a crash.
- having students explain the need for a seat belt in terms of Newton's Laws of Motion.

The use of tobacco increases the risk of illness. Students should understand the influence of short-term social and psychological factors that lead to tobacco use and the possible long-term detrimental effects of smoking and chewing tobacco (NSES, page 168).

Alcohol and other drugs are often abused substances. Such drugs change how the body functions and can lead to addiction (NSES, page 168).

Like other decisions related to personal health, the decision to use drugs, including alcohol and tobacco, is clouded by peer pressure and a young person's perception of invincibility. It is important to explore the science of these issues through group investi-

gations and analysis.

Early adolescents are attacked from all sides. There is considerable pressure from teachers, parents, and the media to avoid drugs—to "Just Say No!" For many of our middle level students there is a voice that is as strong or stronger encouraging them to use tobacco, alcohol, and drugs. The science classroom can serve as a neutral forum to allow students to analyze these messages. With a focus on rational decision-making, science teachers can help their students with a critical analysis of the effects of tobacco, alcohol, and other drugs on their bodies and make knowledgeable decisions about their own behavior.

Teachers can promote these healthy decisions by
- "smoking" cigarettes in a clear detergent bottle filled with cotton balls and comparing the cotton balls from one, five, ten, and twenty cigarettes (note that this activity must be done outside or under a fume hood).
- keeping a class journal of local news stories about accidents that result from drug or alcohol abuse.
- analyzing print, television, and billboard advertising about tobacco, alcohol, and drugs. What claims are companies making in their advertisements? What message are they conveying to early adolescent students?

Sex drive is a natural human

function that requires understanding. Sex is also a prominent means of transmitting diseases. The diseases can be presented through a variety of precautions. (NSES, page 168)

Human sexuality is one of the topics in science that is most likely to raise the concern of parents and the community. Although it would be easy for middle level science teachers to avoid the topic, and hence the possibility of controversy, it is also one of the most critical issues facing early adolescents. Their lives literally depend on their knowledge and the decisions that they will make about their sexuality.

The NSTA Position Statement, The Teaching of Sexuality and Human Reproduction *(NSTA Handbook, 1997–1998,* page 238, Arlington, VA) has the following statements:

"Although few concerns are as fundamental to the affairs of humanity as reproduction and sexuality, the teaching of these subjects continues to be discouraged or actually prohibited in many educational systems. Moreover, even without explicit restrictions, many teachers still must contend with an implied possibility of administrative or community censure."

The position statement goes on to make three specific recommendations:
"**I.** We are concerned with the biological aspects of reproduction and identify the following topics as being properly part of the biological subject matter of human reproduction:
• genetic and endocrine foundations of sexuality
• anatomy and physiology of male and female reproduction systems
• nature and development of secondary sex characteristics
• puberty, menopause, and other sex-related phenomena of the life cycle
• sperm and egg maturation, including the menstrual cycle
• methods of birth control
• development of embryo and fetus, including polyembryony birth, lactation, and postnatal development
• relation of reproduction to population biology and the ecology of man
• reproductive hygiene and the principal reproductive diseases

II. In addition, we consider knowledge of human sexuality to be a fundamental and natural characteristic of humans that is essential in understanding the attitudes and actions of individuals, families, communities, and nations.

Instruction should involve the physical, emotional, mental, and social dimensions of sexuality. It is important that this instruction be related to the maturation of the students and conducted by trained, qualified teachers.

III. We regard instruction in sexuality and the biology of human reproduction to be essential in the education of every person and to represent a legitimate component of any teaching program in the life sciences. We hold that education in this field is feasible at every curricular stage and can, therefore, begin at the earliest grade level."

Decisions about sexual activity are intertwined with social acceptance. Knowledge about their own sexuality, however, is a critical first step in helping students make decisions about the actions that they will take. In addition, understanding the biological imperative of sexual feelings is more likely to result in self-control than not having the knowledge necessary to put powerful feelings into context. Students can recognize, through an understanding of the immune system, that the risk of contracting HIV adds new dimension to the decision of whether to engage in un-protected sex. If young people are to make decisions with their heads and not their hor-mones, they must understand what their hormones are tell-ing them.

There are many activities that teachers can share with their students to provide them with the information to make wise decisions about their sexuality. Among these activi-ties are

• modeling transfer of a sexu-ally transmitted disease in a population. Each member of a class receives a drop-per and a cup of a clear liq-uid (most students receive tap water; one or two re-ceive tap water with phenol-phthalein, an acid-base indicator). Students roam and "exchange fluids" using their dropper. After several minutes of interaction, add a small amount of ammo-nia or another base to each student's cup of liquid. Liq-uids of those who "ex-changed fluids" with those "infected" with the phenol-phthalein will be revealed by the dramatic color change. Relate this activity to the transmission of a dis-ease such as HIV in the population.

• making a chart of those dis-eases that are transmitted through sexual contact. In-clude a description of the nature of the disease, of the organism that causes the disease, symptoms, preven-tion, treatment, and long-term problems associated with the disease.

Natural environments may contain substances (for ex-ample, radon and lead) that are harmful to human beings. Maintaining environmental health involves establishing or monitoring quality standards related to use of soil, water, and air (NSES, page 168).

Understanding the concept that there are natural pollut-ants, such as radon and lead, must start with an exploration of how humans fit into the natural world. Human-cre-ated environments—houses, roads, cars, schools, lawns, parks, shopping malls—are where we modern humans spend most of our time. We spend tremendous amounts of time and money insulating ourselves from the natural Earth processes that produce changes in the weather.

Many middle level stu-dents have probably spent very little time in a setting with few or no human struc-tures. When humans do en-counter such a setting, it is perceived as "natural." What is "unnatural" about human-created environments? Grap-pling with the misconception that human equals unnatural causes students to perceive themselves in a larger biologi-cal and geological picture.

By focusing on under-standing the role of humans in the natural world, students are able to explore environ-mental quality from a new per-spective. Do humans cause everything "bad" or hazardous about the environment? What are our strategies for maintain-ing health through environ-mental quality?

Natural or "human-made"? How we answer this question and see ourselves as a part of the natural world will determine the sustainability of Earth as a life support sys-tem. The generation of young people in our middle schools right now will make this de-termination.

Science teachers can help students develop the knowl-edge to make these decisions through activities such as the following:

• interview local environmen-tal quality officials to find out what natural pollutants occur locally.

• identify a particular study site—a stream or an area of the school yard—to produce an environmental audit. Conduct investigations to determine the levels of pol-lutants in the area and to collect evidence on how humans have impacted this particular environment.

Populations, Resources, and Environments

When an area becomes over-populated, the environment will become degraded due to the increased use of resources (NSES, page 168).

Causes of environmental degradation and resource depletion vary from region to region and from country to country (NSES, page 168).

It is a commonly held misconception that the activities of an individual (or small group) can have little impact upon the environment. Middle school students are not unique in holding this idea. You need merely to look at the litter along a roadside to realize how common the notion is that protection of the environment is someone else's responsibility.

Yet middle school students are at an ideal developmental stage to become aware of their impact upon the environment. They are making a transition from a very self-centered view of the world (what do people think of me?) to an awareness and concern about their relationship to others. Environmentalists speak of "think globally—act locally." Middle school students are poised to make a transition to this kind of thinking. This developing social consciousness is often evident when students move from a concern about what is

fair for them to what is fair for others (first their friends and then the broader community). The involvement of students in service learning projects is a growing movement in middle schools. Projects include visits to nursing homes, tutoring of elementary children, and environmental clean-up activities. Through this action and involvement, middle school students see that they can have a direct and immediate impact on the environment.

Teachers can help middle school students become more aware of their roles and their impact on the environment in a variety of ways, such as the following:
- involve them in action projects that contribute to the community. For example, students might adopt a section of a stream or a bicycle path and be responsible for picking up trash on a regular basis.
- help students to recognize

that pollution is a global issue by examining the pollution produced by different countries. A good case study is the Mexican border industries (maquiladoras) and the impact that those industries have on the quality of life in U.S. and Mexican border cities.
- some of the activities in the National Wildlife Federation program *Project Wild* provide students with graphic illustrations of the effects of overpopulation on land use. "Oh Deer," for example, looks at the impact of shelter, food, and water on the carrying capacity of a region to support a deer population.

Natural Hazards

Internal and external processes of the earth system cause natural hazards, events that change or destroy human and wildlife habitats, damage property, and harm or kill hu-

PHOTODISC

graphic illustration of the idea "out of sight—out of mind." There are numerous examples of the human impact on the environment and the resulting unintended effects. This is especially true in the cases of careless overbuilding on the surface of the Earth, which prevents the replenishment of groundwater.

It is important for students to recognize that environmental decisions have social implications. When a coastal community decides to put in a new marina, it is balancing the economic gains (jobs, business investment) against the potential pollution, loss of habitat, noise, and traffic that would result. Where do we draw the line? This question has consumed politicians, scientists, and community members for years.

This issue can provide an excellent opportunity for engaging students in debate. Set up a scenario. A pristine river runs through a wilderness area. Many people enjoy hunting and fishing on it. One day, a developer announces that he has bought a large tract of land along the river and plans to build a large resort that will include water-skiing on the river in the summer and snow mobiling during the winter. It will mean 500 new jobs for the region (which is quite poor because of a lack of any industry) and an opportunity for new businesses to come into

mans. *Natural hazards include earthquakes, landslides, wildfires, volcanic eruptions, floods, storms, and even possible impacts of asteroids* (NSES, page 168).

These grand, global processes are difficult for students to imagine because it is impossible for teachers to produce relevant "hands-on" activities. Yet the recent abundance of disaster movies focusing on volcanoes, tornadoes, and asteroids has raised the awareness of middle school students to the possibility of these events occurring.

Using case studies, such as the eruption of Mount St. Helen's, demonstrates to middle school students nature's awesome destructiveness as well as the powerful resiliency of life in recovering from these disasters. There are also some excellent films and videos that

show graphic illustrations of volcanic eruptions, such as the eruption of Kilauea in Hawaii, or close-up views of a tornado in action.

Human activities also can induce hazards through resource acquisition, urban growth, land-use decisions, and waste disposal. Such activities can accelerate many natural changes (NSES, page 168).

Natural hazards can present personal and societal challenges because misidentifying the change or incorrectly estimating the rate and scale of change may result in either too little attention and significant human costs or too much cost for unneeded preventative measures (NSES, pages 168–169).

Recently, a large New England city proposed to ship its municipal wastes out to sea for disposal. This became a

the community to service the growing tourist trade.

Divide your class into three groups. One group will represent the interests of the developer. What would be the arguments in favor of supporting this plan? Another group will represent the environmental interests. Why would they prefer to see the environment remain untouched? The third group will represent the town council. They will listen to the presentations from the developers and environmental interests and decide whether to support or deny the permits for the resort. This lively debate can highlight many of the issues while providing students with an opportunity to question their own views and develop good supporting arguments.

A similar instructional unit is available from SEPUP (Science Education for Public Understanding Project) called "Investigating Groundwater: The Fruitvale Story" in which students test water samples to locate the source of groundwater contamination in the fictional town of "Fruitvale," then debate various clean-up options at a simulated town meeting.

Risks and Benefits

Risk analysis considers the type of hazard and estimates the number of people that might be exposed and the number likely to suffer consequences.

Students should understand the risks associated with natural hazards...., chemical hazards..., biological hazards..., social hazards..., and personal hazards.

Individuals can use a systematic approach to thinking critically about risks and benefits.

Important personal and social decisions are made based on perceptions of benefits and risks (NSES, page 169).

According to the National Science Education Standards, there is little research that focuses on students understanding of risk/benefit relationships. Some students will consider risks over which they have no control (for example, hurricanes, viral disease) to be frightening. However, risks that are voluntary (smoking, not using a seat belt) are perceived by some middle school students to be no one else's business. They rebel at authority figures telling them what to do, for example: "Wear your helmet when you are biking."

Another SEPUP unit, "Risk Comparison," focuses on the risks associated with various activities from a mathematical point of view. Students develop decision-making skills as they analyze the probability that an event will cause harm.

Science and Technology in Society

In contrast to pure scientific inquiry, technological design offers solutions that meet human needs, solve problems, or involve the development of new products. Science, however, remains at the heart of technology.

Students' perceptions of science and technology are formed by a number of factors, but perhaps none more powerful than the media. Science and technology are alternatively portrayed as the answer to human problems and as the source of those problems. "A New Discovery about AIDS" heralds one newspaper headline, only to be followed by "Community Pickets Proposed Nuclear Plant" over fears of pollution or worse.

Technology is not perfect. It is often associated with trade-offs in safety, cost, and efficiency. However, as our understanding of science expands, our technological solutions evolve. Many improvements are designed to overcome unintentional consequences and the risks that are coupled with the beneficial aspects of technology. As students observe, perfect solutions do not exist.

At the middle school level, students should have the op-

PHYLLIS DUKE

portunity to consider how the nature of science influences the way in which we look at the world. Although we might not think about it at the time, we are trained to approach problem-solving in a logical manner using scientific methodology. The light bulb will not go on. What are some possible hypotheses? The bulb is burned out. The lamp is unplugged. The power has gone off. We address each in turn until we find a solution—a simple scientific method.

As the nature of science influences society, so too society influences science. Questions that are of concern to society, such as curing AIDS or cleaning up the air, become the focus of scientific investigations and technological ad-

vances. These technological advances, in particular, have had a marked impact on our way of life. Just think what your life would be like without a microwave oven, a telephone, or a computer.

Many people and cultures have contributed to science (see Standard G, *History and Nature of Science* for a more thorough discussion of the role of culture on science). In addition, people who are involved in science and technology work in a variety of settings such as university or business research laboratories, doctors and veterinary offices, chemical and pharmaceutical plants, and consumer researchers in quality control labs at manufacturing plants.

Middle level students need the opportunity to consider case studies of technological and scientific breakthroughs. They should examine the benefits of the breakthroughs as well as the possible negative implications. One structured way to accomplish this is to use an "implications wheel." The breakthrough is put in the middle of the wheel. On the spokes are written the different aspects of society that are likely to be impacted, for example economics, health, environment, and politics. Students then brainstorm the positive and negative implications for each of these areas of society, examining the technology for unexpected consequences.

Habib, Gary, and Anderson, Kathryn, and Hawkins, Cassandra. (1995, February). Science in the Courtroom: A Healthy Diet on Trial. *Science Scope, 18* (5), 16–20.

Harris, Mary E. (1996, April). Water Treatment: Can You Purify Water for Drinking? *Science Scope, 19* (7), 10–12.

Jewett, Jon. (1996, April). Protecting Our Water Resources. *Science Scope, 19* (7), 26–27.

Kazzi, John W. (1996, February). 200 Million Tons of Trash. *Science Scope, 19* (5), 25–26.

McElheny, Mike, Baldwin, Mark, and **Sharp, William.** (1997, May). The Selborne Project: Understanding Natural History in your Community. *Science Scope, 20* (8), 14–17.

Murfin, Brian. (1997, February). Science on the Basketball Floor. *Science Scope, 20* (5), 10–12.

Palmer, Jacqueline. (1992, November/December). The Garbage Game. *Science Scope, 16 (3),* 16–22.

Rivera, Deborah, and Banbury, Mary. (1994, May). Conserving Water: Every Drop Makes a Difference. *Science Scope, 17* (8), 15–19.

Shewell, John A. (1997, May). Petroleum Technology— From Refinery to Home, Business, and Industry. *Science Scope, 20* (8), 25–26.

Sterling, Donna R. (1996, February). Science in the News. *Science Scope, 19* (5), 22–24.

Vandas, Steve, and **Nancy L. Cronin.** (1996, May). Hazardous Waste: Cleanup and Prevention. *Science Scope, 19* (8), 30–31.

Walton, Susan A., and **Lynch, Maurice P.** (1997, May). The Menhaden Mystery. *Science Scope, 20* (8), 10–13.

Weekley, Barbara. (1995, October). What's Bugging You? *Science Scope, 19* (2), 35–36.

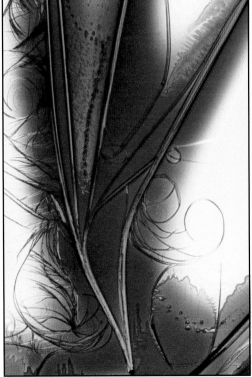

NIKON #13—Crystallized polymer (200x)

Comparison of K–12 NSES Content Standard G: History and Nature of Science

The complete text for the Standard related to History and Nature of Science is found in NSES. Each part of the Standard discussed below is identified by its highlighted main statement.

LEVELS K–4	LEVELS 5–8	LEVELS 9–12
SCIENCE AS A HUMAN ENDEAVOR	**SCIENCE AS A HUMAN ENDEAVOR**	**SCIENCE AS A HUMAN ENDEAVOR**
• Science and technology as having been practiced by people for a long time. • Men and women in science as having achieved much, but with much more to do. • Science as a career for many people.	• Kinds of people engaged in science and engineering and ways they work. • Human capacities and qualities required for science.	• Societal and cultural influences.
• Contributions throughout history.		• Contributing to the scientific enterprise. • Ethical traditions.
	NATURE OF SCIENCE • Normalcy of disagreement in areas of active research. • Importance of evaluating results of scientific inquiry and of open communication among scientists. • Importance of experimentation and observational confirmation in testing and changing ideas in science.	**NATURE OF SCIENTIFIC KNOWLEDGE** • Role of empirical standards, logical arguments, and skepticism. • Criteria for scientific explanations. • Change in scientific knowledge.
	HISTORY OF SCIENCE • Value of studying the contributions of individuals. • Value of looking at science in the history of many peoples. • Challenges for innovators from historical perspectives.	**HISTORICAL PERSPECTIVES** • Historical contributions and growth of modern science. • Advances through daily work of many individuals. • Key advances. • Evolution of knowledge over time.

Content Standard G provides an excellent opportunity for science teachers to collaborate with teachers in other disciplines, particularly the social sciences, to bring science closer to the rest of the curriculum.

The idea of Science as a Human Endeavor is common to the elementary, middle level, and high school standard. Students at the elementary level learn that men and women throughout history have contributed to our present understanding of science, but that there is still much to be learned. They are introduced to male and female role models from various cultures, through books, videos and films. They also learn about different career options in science. This is developed further at the middle school level as the focus shifts to the variety of skills needed by scientists and engineers.

Through their own investigations, students learn about the importance of experimentation and the verification of results. By using examples of historical figures in science and case studies of scientific experiments, teachers can help their students to experience the way in which scientific knowledge develops. At the high school level, students begin to explore the ethical dimensions of science and scientific inquiry as they consider how the scientific community resolves differences of opinion and they learn about the standards by which scientific inquiry is judged.

The study of the history and nature of science offers middle level students a humanistic approach to the appreciation of science and its relationship to society. After being introduced to historical accounts of scientific work, middle level students come to appreciate how early scientists made amazing discoveries—often using only simple tools and making great personal sacrifices. Furthermore, they begin to realize that conclusions we consider obvious today may not have been considered so in the past.

Middle level students, in general, do not have an accurate understanding of the practice of science in either contemporary or historical contexts. Often their images of science and scientists are formed by the media which tends to portray the scientist as a wild-eyed, white male with

PHOTODISC

long hair who is mixing strange chemicals together with little regard for the outcome.

Students need to recognize that scientists often work in teams and even those who work alone must communicate with others for their discoveries to be validated. This becomes an excellent vehicle for teachers to introduce cooperative learning to their classes. Furthermore, to confront students' most common misconceptions about science, it is critical that we use examples that show clearly that the practice of science is open to anyone and requires other qualities in addition to scientific skills.

The authentication of scientific knowledge depends on scientists evaluating the investigations and explanations of other scientists. Students should learn to value skepticism, questioning, and open communication. Toward this end, they should gain practice in reviewing procedures, examining evidence, questioning reasoning processes, making inferences and suggesting alternative explanations for the same evidence. Through these activities, students will discover that it is normal for scientists to disagree with one another about the evidence. When student results differ, they should be given the opportunity to repeat an investigation, reject data that are not within the norm, and eliminate incorrect ideas.

MAX-KARL WINKLER

The Sailors' Scourge

How do you help students to realize that it was real people who contributed to discoveries in science and not just a bunch of names in a textbook? I decided to take my students on a trip back through time. I started with a short video clip from the movie *The Time Machine*, but just as the time machine was about to take off, I stopped the tape.

"What's going on?" came the chorus of responses from the students. "It is time for you to become time-travelers, and your journey is about to begin."

Now that I had their attention, I asked the students what they knew about the disease called scurvy. Students responded that it is caused by a diet that does not have enough Vitamin C (ascorbic acid) and that it can be prevented by eating fresh vegetables and citrus fruits.

Now we were ready for the trip through time. I showed the students a slide of an Eighteenth Century sailing ship. "The year is 1747. You are aboard the sailing ship *HMS Salisbury* traveling from England to the New World colony of Plymouth, Massachussetts." We examined excerpts from a journal of a sailor aboard a ship captained by Magellan to learn about the conditions under which sailors lived.

"We ate ... powder of biscuit, swarming with worms. It stank strongly of the urine of rats... The gums of both the lower and the upper teeth of some of our men swelled so that they could not eat under any circumstances and therefore died... Men lay in the sick bay, suffering from a disease that no one knew how to cure."

A ship's doctor, James Lind, found the answer through experimentation. He divided the sick men into groups of two. The first group

Focusing on students' prior knowledge allows them to develop a conceptual anchor for the new information to be learned.

Case studies and historic documents bring history alive for students.

ate the same basic diet they were used to, with one exception: they received a quart of apple cider each day. The second group was given 25 drops of a strong solution of sulfuric acid and elixir vitriol. The third group took two spoonfuls of vinegar each day. The fourth group was given a mixture of herbs and spices, including nutmeg and garlic. The fifth group drank sea water and the sixth group received two oranges and one lemon each day.

Although Dr. Lind did not know it at the time, the secret to curing scurvy was eating a diet high in Vitamin C.

"All right sailors," I said in my best captain's voice. "You have chosen to join this ship's crew. You will be in charge of the galley. As the ship's cooks, you will work in teams of four to decide which of these foods is highest in Vitamin C. "

The galley crews went to work quickly and spent the rest of the period using the indicator, indophenol, first to determine the ascorbic acid content in two control solutions, and then in the six food samples of Vitamin C which had been diluted to different concentrations. To make the laboratory even more authentic, the test solutions were labeled for the various test foods that Dr. Lind had fed to his crew members.

After the students had finished their investigations, I continued the story. "The group that ate the oranges and lemons was the first to recover. In fact, both sailors recovered within six days. After that, Dr. Lind fed each of the sick men oranges and limes, and soon all were cured of the disease." As an extension, the next day the students continued their investigations to determine the effect of heat on Vitamin C concentration with the challenge of deciding if the foods should be stored above or below deck.

I like this activity as a way to show students how people from many walks of life (yes, even ship doctors in the Eighteenth Century) use scientific reasoning to solve a problem. As a post-lab activity, we talk about the importance of having solutions of known concentration to compare with the (unknown) test solutions. Later, we examine the data from all of the groups for evidence of overall trends or places where errors could have occurred. Finally, the information is converted into graphs so that we can communicate what we found to other students.

Angela Smith, *5th grade science teacher*

> Scientists work in teams and students need experience working in cooperative groups.

> Scientists use experimentation as the primary means for collecting data and comparing results. It is also important that experiments be replicated either by using more than one group or by making repeated observations.

> Students need the opportunity to explore contradictory data and to consider reasons for the differing results.

Science as a Human Endeavor

With so many procedures and principles being addressed in the study of science, the human element is often overlooked. Science is a dynamic process performed by different individuals in many countries around the world. The practice of science is not limited by race, sex, age, or culture. Nor is the practice of science limited to laboratories. Scientific work takes place in a variety of settings, in hospitals, weather stations, tropical rain forests, deserts, manufacturing laboratories, and even on 18th Century sailing ships. Whether working alone or in teams, scientists communicate and share knowledge.

Doing science requires different abilities depending on the field of study, type of inquiry, and cultural context. The practice of science relies on a variety of human qualities. Reasoning, insight, creativity, skepticism, and openness to new ideas are all important attributes in scientists.

Science as a Human Endeavor is best conveyed through day to day instruction which includes examples of the work of men and women of all backgrounds, encourages positive communication among students, models the use of team learning, discusses the importance of human qualities in science, and communicates high expecta-

tions for every science student.

A variety of science activities provide opportunities to emphasize these issues. For example, students can:

- take field trips (real, video, or slide) to various workplaces (hospitals, research labs, and engineering firms) that show workers from all backgrounds doing scientific work.
- interview individuals working in science and technology to find out what personal qualities have been important to them. Find out what attracted them to the field and if they ever thought they would be in their current job when they were in middle school. Ask them if they work independently or as part of a team and why it is important for them to communicate with other scientists.

Another important way to emphasize these issues is to have students mirror the work of scientists. Classroom activities should provide students with many opportunities to work together as diverse teams. Furthermore, the important role that each individual plays, regardless of gender, race, or social background should be emphasized. Groupings should strive for a range of abilities and backgrounds in the individuals in each group and emphasize the important role of each person. The use of structured cooperative groups will provide students with the necessary collaborative skills for

success in working in groups, and define specific roles that the students are to carry out in their groups. By tapping the skills of each team member and by communicating with one another, students will develop a fuller understanding of the work at hand and the way scientists benefit from collective knowledge.

Students should also be provided with opportunities to work independently, explore a variety of questions in their own way, gather information, compare their results to those of others, and develop concepts based on information gathered from a broad spectrum of sources. A vital part of this work is the communication of accurate data and observations based on findings. Students should learn that others can benefit from their work only if their research is accurate and the data and observations are shared.

Nature of Science

The Nature of Science deals with how scientists go about their work. Although asking questions and finding answers is basic science, evaluating differences of opinion and modifying explanations is also part of the scientific process. Scientific ideas arise from inquiry. These ideas must be tested through experiments and observations. Even if similar results are obtained, repeating a procedure helps ensure reliability.

When repeated investigations provide conflicting results, the challenge is to judge whether the differences are significant. Scientists review procedures, examine evidence, provide alternative explanations, and carry out additional experiments as necessary. Even though a hypothesis has been proposed, the evidence may not support it. Scientists acknowledge conflicting views, trusting that future inquiry will resolve the conflict.

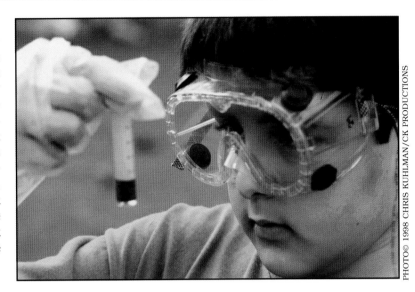

By evaluating processes and evidence continually, scientists promote the evolution of scientific thought. As in the past, new data may change understanding, resulting in the inquiry taking a new direction. On the other hand, some scientific knowledge that is very old and still valid today.

Students need to learn to question their own work and that of other students, as well as the scientific work conducted outside the classroom. Critical analyses of scientific data presented in newspapers, magazines, and advertisements can be useful in showing students how data can be used to promote a particular point of view. Questioning may lead students to repeat an investigation, conduct further investigations, or ask related questions. After conducting investigations individually or in groups, students should compare their data and conclusions with classmates. When differences exist, students should attempt to identify the reasons for the discrepancies. They should determine if the results are valid, if the conclusion is stated correctly, or if the investigation must be repeated. The end result should be a resolution of the discrepancies.

Teachers can help students to analyze scientific data and conclusions critically by:
- asking them to map the location of the major tectonic plates. Have students cut out and fit the continents together. Compare differences in the way in which the students constructed their maps and discuss whether the new map supports the theory that the Earth's crust is composed of moving plates.
- sharing ideas that differ from commonly held beliefs about such current topics as global warming, ozone depletion, the transmission of AIDS, or the origin of the universe. Emphasize how sophisticated technology and the length of time that data have been collected have changed viewpoints of these issues.
- selecting scientific news stories from the gossip newspapers that seem to make fantastic claims ("Boy found with Body of Fish," "President Abducted by Aliens") and have the students make a critical analysis of the science being presented.

History of Science

Scientific contributions have been made by men and women in many cultures, at different times, and in a variety of physical settings. Through case studies and vignettes, history offers a way to learn about the scientific endeavor. Scientific discoveries are influenced by technological advancements and constraints, preconceptions, competition among scientists and corporations, social controversy, available funding, world events, personalities, and events in nature.

By tracing the history of science within a social context, students can learn how difficult it was for some scientific innovators to break through the preconceptions of their time and convince others of their discoveries. Principles we consider to be obvious today may not have been regarded as true in the past.

Since historical studies frequently emphasize revolutions and breakthroughs, we should take care to convey that normal, everyday science is a step-by-step movement toward conclusions. We should not present historical examples as isolated happenings but as microcosms of the nature and inquiry of science—a few moments in a long process, and events that take place in the broad historic context of society.

Through studying historical vignettes and case studies, students will gain a better understanding of the history of science. Stories that oversimplify the scientific endeavor or the individuals involved can distort both science and history and should be avoided. Role models in science should be those individuals who illustrate courage, determination, and unconventional ideas. Appropriate case studies for middle level students can include the lives and work of Galileo, Copernicus, Lavoisier, Dalton, Marie Curie, Pierre Curie, Pasteur, James Watt, and more contemporary scientists such as Jonas Salk and Eugenie Clark.

Students should have the opportunity to learn about several of these scientists by conducting research and reading complete biographies as well as vignettes of their work. The research should focus on the individual's contributions to science and how the culture of the time influenced their work. Students should explore why the scientist's ideas met resistance or were hard to prove. They should also have an opportunities to share what they have learned, either through an oral presentation or a written report.

Activities like the following help to bring science history alive for students.

- have the students make a table listing a variety of facts about a scientist. For example, include race, national origin, nature of work, obstacles overcome, and society's reactions to the work.
- have the class work together on a time line with each student assigned a particular period. As they research, students should find out about the scientists that worked during that period, the discoveries they made, and world events that influenced science and technology during that period.

Alters, Brian J. (1997, January). Whose Nature of Science? *Journal of Research in Science Teaching, 34* (1), 39–55.

Dalton, Edward A. (1997, March). Happy Birthday, Thomas Edison! *Science Scope, 20* (6), 44–45.

Duschl, Richard A. (1994). Research on the History and Philosophy of Science, in Gabel, Dorothy L. (ed.), *Handbook of Research on Science Teaching and Learning*, New York: Macmillian Publishing, 443–465.

Hampton, Elaine, and Gallegos, Charles. (1994, March). Science for All Students. *Science Scope, 17* (6), 5–8.

Mills, Melinda B. (1994, March). Herbal Medicine Along the Trail of Tears. *Science Scope, 17* (6), 36–40.

Small, Parker A., Jr., and Small, Natalie S. (1995, October). Celebrate Immunization! *Science Scope, 19* (2), 33–34.

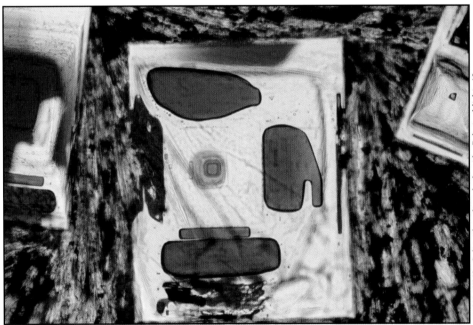

NIKON #HM3—Salt with sodium hydroxide. Polarized light, 40x

First Image of the Global Biosphere

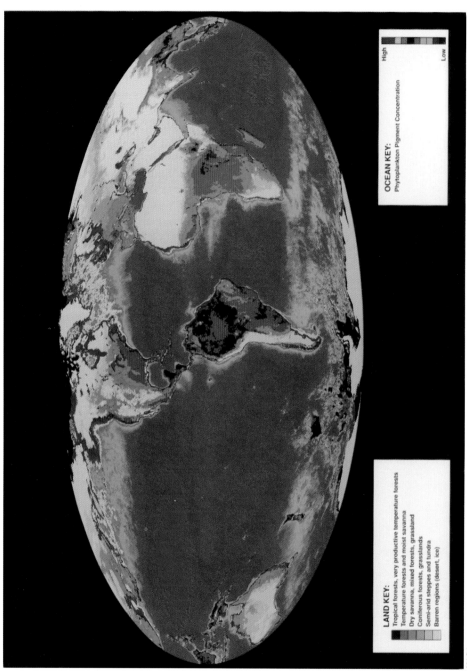

LAND KEY:
Tropical forests, very productive temperature forests
Temperature forests and moist savanna
Dry savanna, mixed forests, grassland
Coniferous forests, grasslands
Semi-arid steppes and tundra
Barren regions (desert, ice)

OCEAN KEY:
Phytoplankton Pigment Concentration

High

Low

NASA

Program Standards

To effect change in programs, we will have to accept positions of leadership in our communities. And to do that, we will have to believe in ourselves.

Moving into the Program Standards

very child is born a scientist. Children have the nonstop curiosity that continually prompts them to compare their internal world with the input of their senses and struggle to make sense of it all. It is the challenge of middle level science to nurture and keep that curiosity alive!

What Makes a Good Science Program?

What does a good science program look like in light of the Standards? The Standards define a good program as one that is designed around student knowledge, skills, and attitudes.

The science program for all middle level students should include all the Content Standards embedded in inquiry-centered curricula that are developmentally appropriate, interesting, and relevant to students' lives. The science program in every classroom must be an integral part of the core academic subjects and be integrated with other subjects. Students will know that science is an important component of their everyday lives.

Inquiry Is Key

From kindergarten through 12th grade, inquiry is the thread that binds science courses and programs together. Teachers should give all students opportunities to engage in and reflect on natural phenomena through inquiry (observing, organizing, experimenting, and communicating). This is the heart of science. The student who learns how to question, explore, find answers, and solve problems is on the path to the wonderful experience of learning!

The Standards call for aligning good teaching, assessment, and systems support to make students' high expectations a reality. They ask program designers to spend time defining student outcomes and to consider how they expect to assess them when they occur. They ask schools to consider what modifications and compensatory education will provide optimal "opportunity to learn" for *all* students. Perhaps most importantly, they ask schools and systems to consider how to support good ideas.

PHOTO© 1998 CHRIS KUHLMAN/CK PRODUCTIONS

The six Program Standards address the following issues:
- is the program consistent? Is it paced at a developmentally appropriate rate?
- curriculum: Does the curriculum connect to other areas of learning and to the students' world?
- mathematics in science: Are the necessary mathematical tools embedded in and integrated into the program?
- resources: Is the program supported by the time, space, and equipment that is necessary for student growth at each level?
- equity and excellence: Does the program put diverse learners on an equal footing?
- schools as communities of learners: Does the faculty and school community support and continually renew the program?

A Consistent Flow

The goals of school programs often change as students move from grade to grade. Today's elementary science demands informational reading, while middle school science builds skills, and secondary science stresses memorization. While individual courses may look coherent, they often seem inconsistent from the perspective of the student.

The Standards challenge school systems to design science programs with consistent goals for student-learning throughout the grade levels. One approach is to emphasize

real-world applications and societal implications to tie coursework together across the grades.

Resources and Opportunity To Learn

We cannot define expectations for students without looking at the conditions necessary for a realistic "opportunities to learn." Appropriate materials, class size, schedules, storage, and classroom space are all essential for inquiry-based learning. These resources become even more crucial when systems are reaching for equity between students of varied abilities and backgrounds.

The physical environment greatly influences the direction and quality of student experiences in science. Communities that want good science programs must support them with facilities that accommodate active exploration, collaboration, and safe investigation. (For more information about setting up facilities for teaching elementary science, see Appendix C.)

The arrangement of the classroom should be flexible so that it can be changed to accommodate various learning activities. There should be adequate space for groups and individuals to work safely. Reference materials should be readily available. Technology should be easily accessible for research, data analyses and instruction.

Inclusion is another factor that affects the design of science classrooms. Most students with physical or learning challenges benefit from heterogeneous class experiences in science. To accommodate them, changes in traditional construction and instruction have to occur.

Teachers have the responsibility of informing themselves and their students about the potential hazards of exploratory science. All safety rules must be followed at all times. Plugs without ground fault interrupters or cabinets without locks must be given attention. Reconfiguring and adding learning space may have to wait until the next round of construction in your

district, but safety hazards cannot be ignored.

Equity: Science for All

Every school program must ensure equity for every child—regardless of gender, background, learning style, or ability. Equal opportunity to learn often requires *unequal* distribution of time and personnel. Minority students may need role models; at-risk students may need extra attention; and students from language-deprived or non-English speaking backgrounds will need additional time and/or staff in order to participate equally in science classroom experiences.

An important issue related to equity is teachers' expectations for their students. Children try to achieve what their teachers (and parents) believe they can achieve. Separating and labeling students tends to convey low expectations to those students and often pro-

duces decreased achievement, limits cooperative learning, and eliminates positive student role models for behavior.

Well-intentioned teachers are often totally unaware of the hidden bias in their techniques. For example, many teachers and parents *expect* more males than females to like and excel in science. This expectation is apparent in classroom observations of questioning, wait-time, assignment of cooperative roles and laboratory tasks, and by textbook examples and visual aids.

Science is most important for boys and girls at the middle level because these are the years in which career paths are being formed. For many students, the middle level years may be the last time that they are exposed to many of the concepts in science. Just as important, however, is the nurturing of positive attitudes toward science. Middle level teachers play a critical role in fostering scientific literacy.

A Community of Learners

The Program Standards describe a new vision for schools: a community of learners that includes students, teachers, parents, administrators, and concerned and interested citizens. Teachers are full partners in this community. They are the ones who see the systemic barriers to change up close. Because of this unique vantage point, they hold important keys to making changes in school programs, and can influence the community.

Bringing About Change

The Standards stress that all science programs should be assessed continuously. Like good classroom assessments, program assessments should be woven into the fabric of the program itself, not artificially imposed from without. Teachers should look for indications that students are moving toward the goals set by the program.

How does a classroom teacher in an average school district try to move his or her program toward the Standards? It may seem simplistic to say "one step at a time," but many innovations fail because they are too ambitious or try to achieve too much without laying adequate groundwork and resources. Take a step; assess; then take the next step.

READY, FIRE, AIM

Change can be a frightening experience. It is difficult to give up our comfort zones and step out into the unknown. But real reform requires this kind of risk-taking. Michael Fullan, a noted educational change writer, points out that the old maxim, "Ready, Aim, Fire," can be a problem for educational reformers. We spend so much time planning and talking that we never get to the change. He offers a new paradigm—Ready, Fire, Aim—in which we take a risk, then revise based upon the lessons learned. To bring about change, teachers will need the confidence to accept leadership roles and the training to effectively carry out those roles. As educators we have had a history of not being politically proactive. That

Questions Along the Road

#1: Where do we want to go?

If the system has not defined consistent goals for *every* course across the curriculum, that is where to begin. Many systems undertaking K–12 program change fail to achieve consistency because they do not start at the beginning—the science that students need to know in order for them to be successful as citizens in a global society. The beginning of a school science program is to be found *not* in the *courses*, but with the *student*. The question is: what should a graduate of the school district's science program need to know and do to function in the highly scientific and technological world of the 21st Century? A good starting point is to look at the Standards. This document represents a broad-based consensus of what constitutes scientific literacy. That, in combination with state frameworks and local district guidelines will form the basis for a quality school program.

When participants in program review agree on what a graduate should know and be able to do, it is time to chart the contributions of each unit or course to the big picture and write course descriptions. Many schools have found that establishing a common language and format for *every* course in the district is invaluable.

Changing programs is hard work. There are two essential bridges for overcoming inertia: one is support from administrators, science supervisors, and peers. The second is that teachers need to know that their work will be appreciated and supported.

#2: Do support systems exist?

Many grand proposals fail when support that was promised does not materialize. A district may rewrite a program with heavy emphasis on laboratory skills, but then give the responsibility for buying the materials to school committees with varying commitment to the program, or to principals who have different priorities.

Perhaps even more damaging is the expectation that a quality science program can appear like magic in a system with few resources, inadequate physical accommodations, and with the expectation that teachers will provide their own materials. The keys to effective and long-lasting changes are consistency and realism.

#3: How are we going to get there?

This is where the practical experience of teachers is crucial because they can identify changes that need to be made—immediately or soon or in the future. For almost every school, the pathway to a better science program includes professional development. This should never be seen as a one-shot cure for ineffective programming. Staff training must occur before, during, and after implementing a new program.

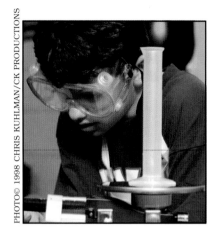

PHOTO© 1998 CHRIS KUHLMAN/CK PRODUCTIONS

time has changed. If we want Standards-based reform to reflect in our curriculum and instructional materials, we must demand that publishers produce appropriate materials. If we want support for new materials and new approaches for Standards-based science teaching, then we must be willing to make our case to administrators, school board members, and legislators.

The pathway to better science programs cannot be taken alone. The professional staff must come together to define their program destination and then chart paths toward goals that parallel and support each another. The Standards provide guiding principles for the journeys teachers must make in their own schools.

RESOURCES FOR THE ROAD

Allen-Sommerville, Lenola. (1994, March). Middle Level Science in a Multicultural Society. *Science Scope, 17* (6), 16–18.

Atwater, Mary M. (1995, October). The Cross-Curricular Classroom. *Science Scope, 19* (2), 42–45.

Carey, Shelley Johnson (Ed.). (1993). *Science for All Cultures.* Arlington, VA: National Science Teachers Association (NSTA).

Dagher, Zoubeida R. (1995, September). Materials Speak Louder than Words. *Science Scope, 19* (1), 48–50.

Luft, Julie A., Bancroft, Jeanne Jones., and **Burketta, Vicki.** (1997, April). An Illuminating View of Mathematics and Science Integration. *Science Scope, 20* (7), 18–21.

Meissner, Donald. (1996, February). Financing Your Hands-On Science Class. *Science Scope, 19* (5), 36.

Melchert, Sandra A. (1996, February). Bidding Basics for Stretching School Science Dollars. *Science Scope, 19* (5), 34–36.

Safety Supplement. (1989, November/December). *Science Scope, 13* (3), S1–S32.

Showalter, Victor M. (1982). *Conditions for Good Science Teaching.* Arlington, VA: National Science Teachers Association (NSTA).

Van Sickle, Meta, and **Dickman, Carolyn.** (1996, November/December). Science Across the Disciplines. *Science Scope, 20* (3), 22–24.

Vos, Robert, and **Pell, Sarah W. J.** (1990, December). Limiting Lab Liability. *The Science Teacher, 57* (9), 34–38.

Yager, Robert E. (1992, November/December). Appropriate Science for All. *Science Scope, 16* (3), 57–59.

Changing Emphases

The National Science Education Standards envision change throughout the system. The Program Standards encompass the following changes in emphases:

LESS EMPHASIS ON	MORE EMPHASIS ON
Developing science programs at different grade levels independently of one another	Coordinating the development of the K–12 science program across grade levels
Using assessments unrelated to curriculum and teaching	Aligning curriculum, teaching, and assessment
Maintaining current resource allocations for books	Allocating resources necessary for hands-on inquiry teaching aligned with the Standards
Textbook- and lecture-driven curriculum	Curriculum that supports the Standards and includes a variety of components, such as laboratories emphasizing inquiry and field trips
Broad coverage of unconnected factual information	Curriculum that includes natural phenomena and science-related social issues that students encounter in everyday life
Treating science as a subject isolated from other school subjects	Connecting science to other school subjects, such as mathematics and social studies
Science learning opportunities that favor one group of students	Providing challenging opportunities for all students to learn science
Limiting hiring decisions to the administration	Involving successful teachers of science in the hiring process
Maintaining the isolation of teachers	Treating teachers as professionals whose work requires opportunities for continual learning and networking
Supporting competition	Promoting collegiality among teachers as a team to improve the school
Teachers as followers	Teachers as decisionmakers

Reprinted with permission from the *National Science Education Standards.* © 1996 National Academy of Sciences. Courtesy of the National Academy Press, Washington, D.C.

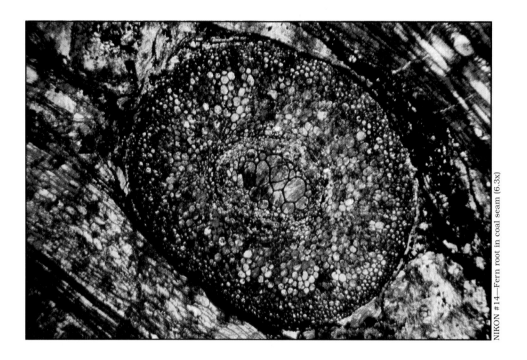

NIKON #14—Fern root in coal seam (6.3x)

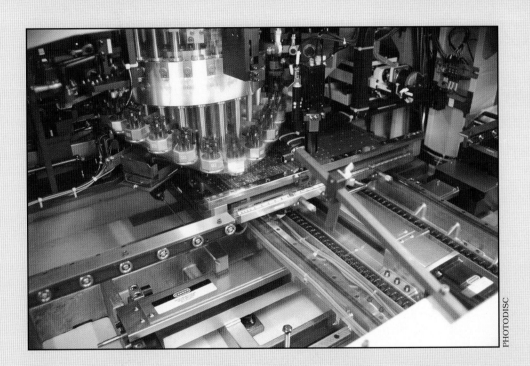

System Standards

All parts of the education system must work together and in the process support us in moving toward the vision of the Standards.

Navigating the System Standards

MYRNA ROBLES

Teachers are the primary movers that will make the Standards real, but they cannot move the mountainous education system toward the Science Standards by themselves. The *Standards* are emphatic on this issue:

"It would be a massive injustice and complete misunderstanding of the Standards if science teachers were left with the full responsibility for implementation. All of the science education community—curriculum developers, superintendents, supervisors, policymakers, assessment specialists, scientists, teacher educators—must act to make the vision of these Standards a reality."

The first step toward any change in education at any level, from the government to the school district to the classroom, is setting the mission. Next, formulating consistent policy at *every* level is critical.

Policies cannot be created and then sent to schools for teachers to implement without supplying adequate resources and support. Policies must be evaluated constantly for intended and unintended consequences. Even with carefully crafted plans, some unexpected effects, both positive and negative, will occur.

All parts of the education system must work *together* and in the process *support* each other in moving toward the vision of the Standards. In this policymaking process, *no* stakeholder can be left out. Teachers, students, administrators, parents, school board members, community members, business and industry representatives, legislators, and representatives of interest groups are *all* important. The Standards provide a common language for all parties to use when talking about the direction science education should take, and in reaching consensus for action.

Prerequisites for Change

In light of these issues, the seven System Standards set out the following prerequisites for changing the education

system to support science education at all levels:

- *Common vision.* Policymakers who influence science education must have a vision that is consistent with the vision of those who coordinate teaching, assessment, professional development, and programs. This vision should also be consistent with the National Science Education Standards.
- *Coordination.* The policies that influence science education should be coordinated across agencies, institutions, and organizations.
- *Continuity.* Policies must be sustained over time so that significant change can be measured against the criteria that have been established.
- *Resources.* Policies must be supported with resources.
- *Equity.* Policies must support equity for all students.
- *Unanticipated effects.* Policies must be examined for possible unintended effects on classroom practice.
- *Individual responsibility.* Responsible individuals will take the opportunity presented by the Standards to move their systems toward reform.

The Power of the Pebble

There are so many components in the education system, that it is easy to feel powerless. But, like the ever-widening ripples formed when a single pebble is dropped into a pond, the efforts of individual teachers can have a multiplying effect on colleagues, students, and parents. Even a single change in a school science program can affect many other areas in ways no one can predict, and every contribution, no matter how small, can make a difference.

Middle level teachers and their principals and supervisors should never consider the size of the task as an excuse for not starting reform. There are simple, proven ways to foster change in *every* system and *every* school and classroom.

School reform takes time. The work is best done in teams. A team might be made up of a group of teachers, the principal, district supervisors, parents, students, and community representatives. A good beginning might be the sharing of the importance of science and the vision of the National Science Education Standards.

The Principal Resource

Educating principals about the importance of science (you

might begin by sharing this book with them!) can turn principals into advocates for science. Principals working with teachers can set realistic goals, address concerns, and provide time, resources, and training. To spark interest, teachers might invite principals and administrators to take part in science lessons with students or to attend a convention to learn what is possible in middle level science. Principals should be invited to join in preparations for science nights, field trips, and similar events.

Bring Parents to School

Parent involvement is a gold mine for a science program. Parents can be recruited as classroom science instructors, bringing their special expertise, or to provide an extra pair of hands, prepare materials, assist during science

lessons, help with clean-up, and go on field trips.

Parents are also resources for gaining publicity for the school's science program. They can help locate resources, science materials and supplies; serve as guest speakers if they work in science-related fields; help run a school- or district-wide science event; identify local businesses that might be interested in becoming involved in the science program; monitor experiments; and raise money for equipment. The list is endless.

Parents can help their children directly by carrying out investigations, watching videotapes, or listening to audiotapes about science topics. Teachers can develop guidelines for parents to direct discussions about the tapes.

When parents are involved in projects with schools and communities, partnerships

are forged that maximize resources and increase support for science. (It is difficult to criticize anything with which you are involved.)

Partner with the Community

Involving community members, including local business people, in the science program also reaps great rewards. Schools may invite business partners to work together to expand an existing science program. Publicity for the business goes a long way in convincing them to join the effort. Businesses may be willing to donate science equipment, mentor students in special projects, or take part in science events. Given the nature of business, the possibilities for cooperation are many.

Middle schools are also adopting service learning as an exciting way to involve their students in the life of their community. Internship experiences with science-re-lated businesses, environmental clean-up projects, and tutoring of younger students can all help middle school children develop an understanding of the role of science in their lives as well as their role in their community.

Connecting With Reform

The Carnegie Council on Adolescent Development released in 1989 the ground-breaking study of middle schools, *Turning Points: Preparing American Youth for the 21st Century.* The Carnegie report makes eight powerful recommendations:

- **Create small communities for learning** in which stable, close, mutually respectful relationships with adults and peers are considered fundamental for intellectual development and personal growth.
- **Teach a core academic program** that produces students who are literate, including the sciences, and who know how to think critically, lead a healthy life, behave ethically, and assume the responsibilities of citizenship in a pluralistic society. Youth service to promote values for citizenship is an essential part of the core academic program.
- **Ensure success for all students** by eliminating tracking and promoting cooperative learning, flexible instructional time, and adequate resources (time, space, equipment, and materials) for teachers.
- **Empower teachers and administrators** to make decisions about the experiences of middle grade students through creative control over the instructional program linked to greater responsibilities for student's performance; establishing governance committees that assist the principal in designing and coordinating school-wide programs; and promoting autonomy and leadership with sub-schools or houses to create environments enhancing the intellectual and emotional development of all youth.
- **Staff middle schools with expert teachers of young adolescents** who have been specifically prepared for assignment to the middle grades.
- **Improve academic performance** by fostering the health and fitness of young adolescents, by providing a health coordinator in every middle school, access to health care and counseling services, and a health-promoting school environment.
- **Re-engage families** in the

It's Your Turn

Eventually, an opportunity will come to a system near you—an issue, a controversy, or the chance to make a significant change in the way science is taught in *your* school. The challenge may come from a pressure group, from parents, or, ideally, from the message of the National Science Education Standards. What practical steps can you take to be part of the process of change?

Rely on Research

Share this book and others with those who make decisions. NSTA also offers an awareness kit for administrators on the National Science Education Standards; another kit is available for teachers.

Bring Friends Along

Convince colleagues of the importance of activism. As a team, share information and insights.

Network on the Net

Access teacher forums (NSTA home page or the World Wide Web) for quick answers to difficult questions in systemic reform.

Maintain Professional Memberships

A major activity of professional organizations is speaking out on issues important to members, and providing information to these members to be more effective advocates of change.

Call for Support

If an issue comes before the school board that is so detrimental or so difficult to combat that it threatens good science education, send out a call for help. Your state science supervisor, your NSTA District or Division Director, or your other professional associations can find expert help for you in your area.

Like the ripples caused by a small pebble, so the involvement of a single teacher can change the system. Given that, imagine the impact of the entire profession speaking with one voice!

education of young adolescents by giving them meaningful roles in school governance, communicating with families about the school program and their student's progress, and offering families opportunities to support the learning process at home and at school.
*   **Connect schools with communities,** which together share responsibility for each middle grade student's success. Identify service opportunities in the community, establish partnerships, and ensure students' access to health and social services. Use community resources to enrich the instructional program and opportunities for constructive after-school activities.

These recommendations sound very similar to those echoed in the *National Science Education Standards.* It is this unity of direction between the Standards and general middle school reform efforts, such as *Turning Points,* that holds the greatest promise for the success of reform at the middle level.

Becoming Active

Ultimately, efforts to change the system must reach beyond individual classrooms and schools. Resisting the old impulse to shut their classroom doors, many teachers are writing and speaking out when proposed changes affect them and their students. The issues that concern them are wide-ranging and include the necessity for providing science teaching materials, federal support for professional development for teachers, and the education of disadvantaged children. Around the nation teachers are running for public office and are using the media to tell the story of school science from their own, unique perspective.

RESOURCES FOR THE ROAD

Baumann, Lorrie, and **Ribeiro, Mary.** (1997, March). Science Alliance. *Science Scope, 20* (6), 19–21.

Ibarra, Hector. (1997, March). Winning Partnership Strategies. *Science Scope, 20* (6), 78–81.

Partnership Possibilities [series of articles in Special Issue: Science in Nontradi-tional Setting]. (1995, March). *Science Scope, 18* (6), 5–28.

Redmond, Alan. (1997, March). Putting Children First. *Science Scope, 20* (3), 4–6, 9.

Torri, Geno. (1997, March). Museum Partnerships. *Science Scope, 20* (3), 58–59.

Tucker, Meg, Seluke, Suzi, and **Tucker, Allen.** (1997, March). Networking a Community of Learners. *Science Scope, 20* (3), 68–69, 71–72.

White, Michael, and **Brown, Donna.** (1997, March). An Industrial–Strength Partnership. *Science Scope, 20* (3), 26–30.

Changing Emphases
District System

LESS EMPHASIS ON	MORE EMPHASIS ON
Technical, short-term, inservice workshops	Ongoing professional development to support teachers
Policies unrelated to Standards-based reform	Policies designed to support changes called for in the Standards
Purchase of textbooks based on traditional topics	Purchase or adoption of curriculum aligned with the Standards and on a conceptual approach to science teaching, including support for hands-on science materials
Standardized tests and assessments unrelated to Standards-based program and practices	Assessments aligned with the Standards
Administration determining what will be involved in improving science education	Teacher leadership in improvement of science education
Authority at upper levels of educational system	Authority for decisions at level of implementation
School board ignorance of science education program	School board support of improvements aligned with the Standards
Local union contracts that ignore changes in curriculum, instruction, and assessment	Local union contracts that support improvements indicated by the Standards

Reprinted with permission from the *National Science Education Standards.* © 1996 National Academy of Sciences. Courtesy of the National Academy Press, Washington, D.C.

Appendices

Appendix A

National Science Education Standards: Some Relevant History

The publication of the *National Science Education Standards* in December 1995 propelled science education into a new and challenging era. Never before has the practice of science education in the United States been guided by a single set of principles reached by national consensus. The *National Science Education Standards* take their place as a significant contribution to the broad reform movement currently under way in American education.

Precursors to Reform

In April 1983, *A Nation at Risk,* thought to be the most important reform publication of this century, warned that if our education system continued to produce citizens illiterate in science, mathematics, and technology, the nation would lose its influential position in the world, becoming a second-rate power in the 21st century. *A Nation at Risk* sparked a wealth of studies and other efforts that eventually coalesced into a significant broad-based reform movement in education.

Among the first studies were efforts to compare the literacy levels of U.S. students with those of students in other countries. Although many of the studies were poorly designed, making their findings invalid, the better studies consistently found a need to improve the teaching of science and mathematics in this country.

Launching Reform

Among the various efforts to reform science education was Project 2061, initiated in 1986 by the American Association for the Advancement of Science. This project takes a long-term view of science education reform. The project's goal is to develop a high level of science literacy among all American citizens. Its first publication, *Science for All Americans* (1989), outlined the understanding and habit of mind necessary for a scientifically literate citizen. In 1993, Project 2061 released *Benchmarks for Science Literacy,* which established minimum goals for what students should know and be able to do at various grade levels in a number of content areas.

In 1989, NSTA launched its Scope, Sequence, and Coordination of Secondary School Science project (SS&C). The NSTA curriculum reform project sought to revamp the layercake approach to the study of science (a different science every year). Instead, a curriculum based on the principles of SS&C would give students carefully sequenced (from concrete to abstract, paralleling student development), well-coordinated instruction in *all* the sciences *every* year. The SS&C approach is currently being field-tested at the high school level. Previous efforts focused on the middle grades. Publications of this project include *The Content Core, Relevant Research,* and *A High School Framework for Science Education.*

Goals and Standards

While these efforts were going on, two other events were propelling the nation toward setting Standards for school subjects. In 1989, after three years of work, the National Council of Teachers of Mathematics released its *Curriculum and Evaluation Standards for School Mathematics*. Its goal was to revolutionize the teaching of mathematics as a subject for *all* students, not just those who were college-bound.

About the same time President Bush decided to convene an education summit of the nation's governors. From this summit came an agreement that national goals for education should be set. The National Governors' Association and the President developed the National Education Goals, which were released in the State of the Union address in early 1990. According to Goal 4, "By the year 2000, U.S. students will be first in the world in science and mathematics achievement."

The National Education Goals Panel was established to monitor progress toward each of the goals. President Bush launched the America 2000 effort to get communities involved in working toward the goals. (Later, President Clinton would continue these goal-directed efforts, renaming the program Goals 2000.)

The need to set *voluntary* national Standards for what all students should know and be able to do at various grade levels in the subjects addressed by the goals soon became apparent. These included science, mathematics, English, history, civics and government, geography, economics, foreign languages, and the arts. Standards-setting projects, often with funding from agencies of the federal government, were quickly launched in these subjects, including science.

Toward Consensus in Science

In spring 1991, the president of NSTA, with the unanimous support of the NSTA board of directors, wrote to Frank Press, president of the National Academy of Sciences and chair of the National Research Council (NRC), asking NRC to coordinate the development of national Standards in science education. The presidents of other leading science and science education associations, the U.S. Secretary of Education, the assistant director for education and human resources at the National Science Foundation (NSF), and the co-chairs of the National Education Goals Panel also encouraged NRC to play a leading role. NRC agreed; and shortly thereafter, major funding for the project was provided by the Department of Education and NSF. Other funders included NASA, the U.S. Department of Energy, the U.S. Department of Agriculture, and the National Institutes of Health.

NRC began its work by convening the National Committee on Science Education Standards and Assessment and the Chair's Advisory Committee, consisting of representatives from the major science and science education associations. This group helped to identify and to recruit staff and volunteers for all the Standards-writing working groups.

The three working groups—content Standards, teaching Standards, and assessment Standards—set to work in summer 1992 and over the next 18 months, solicited input from large numbers of teachers, scientists, science educators, and many others interested in science education.

In spring 1993, a pre-draft of the Science Education Standards was released to selected focus groups for critique and review. Comments were collated and analyzed; and in December 1994, more than 40,000 copies of the draft *National Science Education Standards* were distributed nationwide to some 18,000 individuals and 250 groups. Again, comments were collated and analyzed, and the *National Science Education Standards* was published in December 1995.

The Science Standards provide a vision, *not* a curriculum, for science education. They are descriptive, *not* prescriptive. One of the strongest principles underlying the Standards is that science is for *all* students in all grades.

Release of the *National Science Education Standards* is a pivotal event for teachers of science and those they work with—from students and parents to administrators and legislators. The Standards present clearly what *can* be done but leave the nuts and bolts of implementation to individual choice and responsibility. The *Standards* clearly state that all the Standards should be taken together as a package—implementation should not be done cafeteria-style. And finally, the responsibility for putting the vision of the Standards into action belongs to *everyone* in science education: teachers, curriculum developers, superintendents, administrators, supervisors, policymakers, assessment specialists, scientists, teacher educators, parents, businesses, and local communities.

RESOURCES FOR THE ROAD   History

American Association for the Advancement of Science (AAAS), Project 2061. (1989). *Science for All Americans.* New York: Oxford University Press.

American Association for the Advancement of Science (AAAS), Project 2061. (1993). *Benchmarks for Science Literacy.* New York: Oxford University Press.

Aldridge, Bill G. (Ed.) (1996). *Scope, Sequence, and Coordination: A High School Framework for Science Education.* Arlington, VA: National Science Teachers Association (NSTA).

National Commission on Excellence in Education. (1983). *A Nation at Risk: The Imperative for Educational Reform.* Washington, DC: Author.

National Council of Teachers of Mathematics (NCTM). (1989). *Curriculum and Evaluation Standards for School Mathematics.* Reston, VA: Author.

National Council of Teachers of Mathematics (NCTM). (1989). *Professional Standards for Teaching Mathematics.* Reston, VA: Author.

National Science Teachers Association (NSTA) (1993). *Scope, Sequence and Coordination of Secondary School Science. Vol. I. The Content Core: A Guide for Curriculum Designers.* (Rev. ed.). Arlington, VA: Author.

National Science Teachers Association (NSTA). (1992). *Scope, Sequence, and Coordination of Secondary School Science. Vol. II. Relevant Research,* Arlington, VA: Author.

Appendix B
National Science Education Standards

Principles

- Science is for all students.
- Learning science is an active process.
- School science reflects the intellectual and cultural traditions that characterize the practice of contemporary science.
- Improving science education is part of systemic education reform.

Science Teaching Standards

TEACHING STANDARD A: Teachers of science plan an inquiry-based science program for their students. In doing this, teachers
- Develop a framework of year-long and short-term goals for students.
- Select science content and adapt and design curricula to meet the interests, knowledge, understanding, abilities, and experiences of students.
- Select teaching and assessment strategies that support the development of student understanding and nurture a community of science learners.
- Work together as colleagues within and across disciplines and grade levels.

TEACHING STANDARD B: Teachers of science guide and facilitate learning. In doing this, teachers
- Focus and support inquiries while interacting with students.
- Orchestrate discourse among students about scientific ideas.
- Challenge students to accept and share responsibility for their own learning.
- Recognize and respond to student diversity and encourage all students to participate fully in science learning.

- Encourage and model the skills of scientific inquiry, as well as the curiosity, openness to new ideas and data, and skepticism that characterize science.

TEACHING STANDARD C: Teachers of science engage in ongoing assessment of their teaching and of student learning. In doing this, teachers
- Use multiple methods and systematically gather data about student understanding and ability.
- Analyze assessment data to guide teaching
- Guide students in self-assessment.
- Use student data, observations of teaching, and interactions with colleagues to reflect on and improve teaching practice.
- Use student data, observations of teaching, and interactions with colleagues to report student achievement and opportunities to learn to students, teachers, parents, policymakers, and the general public.

TEACHING STANDARD D: Teachers of science design and manage learning environments that provide students with the time, space, and resources needed for learning science. In doing this, teachers
- Structure the time available so that students are able to engage in extended investigations.
- Create a setting for student work that is flexible and supportive of science inquiry
- Ensure a safe working environment
- Make the available science tools, materials, media, and technological resources accessible to students.
- Identify and use resources outside the school.
- Engage students in designing the learning environment.

TEACHING STANDARD E: Teachers of science develop communities of science learners that reflect the intellectual rigor of scientific inquiry and the attitudes and social values conducive to science learning. In doing this, teachers

- Display and demand respect for the diverse ideas, skills, and experiences of all students.
- Enable students to have a significant voice in decisions about the content and context of their work and require students to take responsibility for the learning of all members of the community.
- Nurture collaboration among students.
- Structure and facilitate ongoing formal and informal discussion based on a shared understanding of rules of scientific discourse.
- Model and emphasize the skills, attitudes, and values of scientific inquiry.

TEACHING STANDARD F: Teachers of science actively participate in the ongoing planning and development of the school science program. In doing this, teachers

- Plan and develop the school science program.
- Participate in decisions concerning the allocation of time and other resources to the science program.
- Participate fully in planning and implementing professional growth and development strategies for themselves and their colleagues.

Standards for Professional Development for Teachers of Science

PROFESSIONAL DEVELOPMENT STANDARD A: Professional development for teachers of science requires learning essential science content through the perspectives and methods of inquiry. Science learning experiences for teachers must

- Involve teachers in actively investigating phenomena that can be studied scientifically, interpreting results, and making sense of findings consistent with currently accepted scientific understanding.
- Address issues, events, problems, or topics significant in science and of interest to participants.
- Introduce teachers to scientific literature, media, and technological resources that expand their science knowledge and their ability to access further knowledge.
- Build on the teacher's current science understanding, ability, and attitudes.
- Incorporate ongoing reflection on the process and outcomes of understanding science through inquiry.
- Encourage and support teachers in efforts to collaborate.

PROFESSIONAL DEVELOPMENT STANDARD B: Professional development for teachers of science requires integrating knowledge of science, learning, pedagogy, and students; it also requires applying that knowledge to science teaching. Learning experiences for teachers of science must

- Connect and integrate all pertinent aspects of science and science education.
- Occur in a variety of places where effective science teaching can be illustrated and modeled, permitting teachers to struggle with real situations and expand their knowledge and skills in appropriate contexts.
- Address teachers' needs as learners and build on their current knowledge of science content, teaching, and learning.
- Use inquiry, reflection, interpretation of research, modeling, and guided practice to build understanding and skill in science teaching.

PROFESSIONAL DEVELOPMENT STANDARD C: Professional development for teachers of science requires building understanding and ability for lifelong learning. Professional development activities must

- Provide regular, frequent opportunities for individual and collegial examination and reflection on classroom and institutional practice.
- Provide opportunities for teachers to receive feedback about their teaching and to understand, analyze, and apply that feedback to improve their practice.
- Provide opportunities for teachers to learn and use various tools and techniques for self-reflection and collegial reflection, such as peer coaching, portfolios, and journals.
- Support the sharing of teacher expertise by preparing and using mentors, teacher advisors, coaches, lead teachers, and resource

teachers to provide professional development opportunities.
- Provide opportunities to know and have access to existing research and experiential knowledge.
- Provide opportunities to learn and use the skills of research to generate new knowledge about science and the teaching and learning of science.

PROFESSIONAL DEVELOPMENT STANDARD D: Professional development programs for teachers of science must be coherent and integrated. Quality preservice and inservice programs are characterized by
- Clear, shared goals based on a vision of science learning, teaching, and teacher development congruent with the *National Science Education Standards.*
- Integration and coordination of the program components so that understanding and ability can be built over time, reinforced continuously, and practiced in a variety of situations.
- Options that recognize the developmental nature of teacher professional growth and individual and group interests, as well as the needs of teachers who have varying degrees of experience, professional expertise, and proficiency.
- Collaboration among the people involved in programs, including teachers, teacher educators, teacher unions, scientists, administrators, policymakers, members of professional and scientific organizations, parents, and businesspeople, with clear respect for the perspectives and expertise of each.
- Recognition of the history, culture, and organization of the school environment.
- Continuous program assessment that captures the perspectives of all those involved, uses a variety of strategies, focuses on the process and effects of the program, and feeds directly into program improvement and evaluation.

Standards for Assessment in Science Education

ASSESSMENT STANDARD A: Assessments must be consistent with the decisions they are designed to inform.
- Assessments are deliberately designed.
- Assessments have explicitly stated purposes.
- The relationship between the decisions and the data is clear.
- Assessment procedures are internally consistent.

ASSESSMENT STANDARD B: Achievement and opportunity to learn science must be assessed.
- Achievement data collected focus on the science content that is most important for students to learn.
- Opportunity-to-learn data collected focus on the most powerful indicators.
- Equal attention must be given to the assessment of opportunity to learn and to the assessment of student achievement.

ASSESSMENT STANDARD C: The technical quality of the data collected is well matched to the decisions and actions taken on the basis of their interpretation.
- The feature that is claimed to be measured is actually measured.
- Assessment tasks are authentic.
- An individual student's performance is similar on two or more tasks that claim to measure the same aspect of student achievement.
- Students have adequate opportunity to demonstrate their achievements.
- Assessment tasks and methods of presenting them provide data that are sufficiently stable to lead to the same decisions if used at different times.

ASSESSMENT STANDARD D: Assessment practices must be fair.
- Assessment tasks must be reviewed for the use of stereotypes, for assumptions that reflect the perspectives or experiences of a particular group, for language that might be offensive to a particular group, and for other features that might distract students from the intended task.
- Large-scale assessments must use statistical techniques to identify potential bias among subgroups.
- Assessment tasks must be appropriately

modified to accommodate the needs of students with physical disabilities, learning disabilities, or limited English proficiency.
- Assessment tasks must be set in a variety of contexts, be engaging to students with different interests and experiences, and must not assume the perspective or experience of a particular gender, racial, or ethnic group.

ASSESSMENT STANDARD E: The inferences made from assessments about student achievement and opportunity to learn must be sound.
- When making inferences from assessment data about student achievement and opportunity to learn science, explicit reference needs to be made to the assumptions on which the inferences are based.

Science Content Standards

Content Standard: K–12

Unifying Concepts and Processes

STANDARD: As a result of activities in grades K–12, all students should develop understanding and abilities aligned with the following concepts and processes:
- Systems, order, and organization.
- Evidence, models, and explanation.
- Constancy, change, and measurement.
- Evolution and equilibrium.
- Form and function.

Content Standards: K–4

Science as Inquiry

CONTENT STANDARD A: As a result of activities in grades K–4, all students should develop
- Abilities necessary to do scientific inquiry.
- Understanding about scientific inquiry.

Physical Science

CONTENT STANDARD B: As a result of the activities in grades K–4, all students should develop an understanding of
- Properties of objects and materials.
- Position and motion of objects.
- Light, heat, electricity, and magnetism.

Life Science

CONTENT STANDARD C: As a result of activities in grades K–4, all students should develop understanding of
- The characteristics of organisms.
- Life cycles of organisms.
- Organisms and environments.

Earth and Space Science

CONTENT STANDARD D: As a result of their activities in grades K–4, all students should develop an understanding of
- Properties of earth materials.
- Objects in the sky.
- Changes in earth and sky.

Science and Technology

CONTENT STANDARD E: As a result of activities in grades K–4, all students should develop
- Abilities of technological design.
- Understanding about science and technology.
- Abilities to distinguish between natural objects and objects made by humans.

Science in Personal and Social Perspectives

CONTENT STANDARD F: As a result of activities in grades K–4, all students should develop understanding of
- Personal health.
- Characteristics and changes in populations.
- Types of resources.
- Changes in environments.
- Science and technology in local challenges.

History and Nature of Science

CONTENT STANDARD G: As a result of activities in grades K–4, all students should develop understanding of
- Science as a human endeavor.

Content Standards: 5–8

Science as Inquiry

CONTENT STANDARD A: As a result of activities in grades 5–8, all students should develop
- Abilities necessary to do scientific inquiry.
- Understandings about scientific inquiry.

Physical Science

CONTENT STANDARD B: As a result of their activities in grades 5–8, all students should develop an understanding of
- Properties and changes of properties in matter.
- Motions and forces.
- Transfer of energy.

Life Science

CONTENT STANDARD C: As a result of their activities in grades 5–8, all students should develop understanding of
- Structure and function in living systems.
- Reproduction and heredity.
- Regulation and behavior.
- Populations and ecosystems.
- Diversity and adaptations of organisms.

Earth and Space Science

CONTENT STANDARD D: As a result of their activities in grades 5–8, all students should develop an understanding of
- Structure of the earth system.
- Earth's history.
- Earth in the solar system.

Science and Technology

CONTENT STANDARD E: As a result of activities in grades 5–8, all students should develop
- Abilities of technological design.
- Understandings about science and technology.

Science in Personal and Social Perspectives

CONTENT STANDARD F: As a result of activities in grades 5–8, all students should develop understanding of
- Personal health.
- Populations, resources, and environments.
- Natural hazards.
- Risks and benefits.
- Science and technology in society.

History and Nature of Science

CONTENT STANDARD G: As a result of activities in grades 5–8, all students should develop understanding of
- Science as a human endeavor.

- Nature of science.
- History of science.

Content Standards: 9–12

Science as Inquiry

CONTENT STANDARD A: As a result of activities in grades 9–12, all students should develop
- Abilities necessary to do scientific inquiry.
- Understandings about scientific inquiry.

Physical Science

CONTENT STANDARD B: As a result of their activities in grades 9–12, all students should develop an understanding of
- Structure of atoms.
- Structure and properties of matter.
- Chemical reactions.
- Motions and forces.
- Conservation of energy and increase in disorder.
- Interactions of energy and matter.

Life Science

CONTENT STANDARD C: As a result of their activities in grades 9–12, all students should develop understanding of
- The cell.
- Molecular basis of heredity.
- Biological evolution.
- Interdependence of organisms.
- Matter, energy, and organization in living systems.
- Behavior of organisms.

Earth and Space Science

CONTENT STANDARD D: As a result of their activities in grades 9–12, all students should develop an understanding of
- Energy in the earth system.
- Geochemical cycles.
- Origin and evolution of the earth system.
- Origin and evolution of the universe.

Science and Technology

CONTENT STANDARD E: As a result of activities in grades 9–12, all students should develop
- Abilities of technological design.

- Understandings about science and technology.

Science in Personal and Social Perspectives

CONTENT STANDARD F: As a result of activities in grades 9–12, all students should develop understanding of
- Personal and community health.
- Population growth.
- Natural resources.
- Environmental quality.
- Natural and human-induced hazards.
- Science and technology in local, national, and global challenges.

History and Nature of Science

CONTENT STANDARD G: As a result of activities in grades 9–12, all students should develop understanding of
- Science as a human endeavor.
- Nature of scientific knowledge.
- Historical perspectives.

Science Education Program Standards

PROGRAM STANDARD A: All elements of the K–12 science program must be consistent with the other *National Science Education Standards* and with one another and developed within and across grade levels to meet a clearly stated set of goals.
- In an effective science program, a set of clear goals and expectations for students must be used to guide the design, implementation, and assessment of all elements of the science program.
- Curriculum frameworks should be used to guide the selection and development of units and courses of study.
- Teaching practices need to be consistent with the goals and curriculum frameworks.
- Assessment policies and practices should be aligned with the goals, student expectations, and curriculum frameworks.
- Support systems and formal and informal expectations of teachers must be aligned with the goals, student expectations, and curriculum frameworks.
- Responsibility needs to be clearly defined

for determining, supporting, maintaining, and upgrading all elements of the science program.

PROGRAM STANDARD B: The program of study in science for all students should be developmentally appropriate, interesting, and relevant to students' lives; emphasize student understanding through inquiry; and be connected with other school subjects.
- The program of study should include all of the content standards.
- Science content must be embedded in a variety of curriculum patterns that are developmentally appropriate, interesting, and relevant to students' lives.
- The program of study must emphasize student understanding through inquiry.
- The program of study in science should connect to other school subjects.

PROGRAM STANDARD C: The science program should be coordinated with the mathematics program to enhance student use and understanding of mathematics in the study of science and to improve student understanding of mathematics.

PROGRAM STANDARD D: The K–12 science program must give students access to appropriate and sufficient resources, including quality teachers, time, materials and equipment, adequate and safe space, and the community.
- The most important resource is professional teachers.
- Time is a major resource in a science program.
- Conducting scientific inquiry requires that students have easy, equitable, and frequent opportunities to use a wide range of equipment, materials, supplies, and other resources for experimentation and direct investigation of phenomena.
- Collaborative inquiry requires adequate and safe space.
- Good science programs require access to the world beyond the classroom.

PROGRAM STANDARD E: All students in the K–12 science program must have equitable access to opportunities to achieve the *National Science Education Standards*.

PROGRAM STANDARD F: Schools must work as communities that encourage, support, and sustain teachers as they implement an effective science program.

- Schools must explicitly support reform efforts in an atmosphere of openness and trust that encourages collegiality.
- Regular time needs to be provided and teachers encouraged to discuss, reflect, and conduct research around science education reform.
- Teachers must be supported in creating and being members of networks of reform.
- An effective leadership structure that includes teachers must be in place.

Science Education System Standards

SYSTEM STANDARD A: Policies that influence the practice of science education must be congruent with the program, teaching, professional development, assessment, and content standards while allowing for adaptation to local circumstances.

SYSTEM STANDARD B: Policies that influence science education should be coordinated within and across agencies, institutions, and organizations.

SYSTEM STANDARD C: Policies need to be sustained over sufficient time to provide the continuity necessary to bring about the changes required by the *Standards*.

SYSTEM STANDARD D: Policies must be supported with resources.

SYSTEM STANDARD E: Science education policies must be equitable.

SYSTEM STANDARD F: All policy instruments must be reviewed for possible unintended effects on the classroom practice of science education.

SYSTEM STANDARD G: Responsible individuals must take the opportunity afforded by the standards-based reform movement to achieve the new vision of science education portrayed in the *Standards*.

Appendix C
Designing Middle School Science Facilities

Program Standard D: *The K–12 science program must give students access to appropriate and sufficient resources, including quality teachers, time, materials and equipment, adequate and safe space, and the community.*

Proper facilities are the foundation for effective science investigations and instruction and essential for providing a safe science learning environment. No curriculum, discipline, or instructional strategy can fully overcome limitations resulting from inadequate facilities.

Middle school students need concrete experiences with scientific phenomena to understand basic science concepts. The *National Science Education Standards* calls time, space, and materials "critical components" for promoting sustained inquiry.

Inductive inquiry/discovery and deductive laboratory and field activities require similar facilities and equipment. The middle school science room is typically a combination laboratory/classroom, but some schools provide separate laboratories.

In planning for either kind of facility, safety, flexibility, and other needs and requirements must be taken into account. The following sections offer several criteria for creating a science learning environment that encourages maximum student involvement and achievement and assists teachers in their work toward achieving the Standards.

Class Time

It is important to allot sufficient time for hands-on inquiry and activities and for accompanying discussion and explanation of the science concepts involved. Plan for a minimum of 250 minutes per week of science instruction in grades 6–8, with at least 60 percent of that time devoted to inquiry/hands-on experiences.

Planning for Facilities Design

Planning involves discussion, investigation, and decisionmaking to determine the physical environment that the science program requires. A participatory process that encourages input from diverse groups is most likely to result in a facility design that is specific to the district, curriculum, and program and benefits from community support.

Before decisions on design and location of science facilities are made, it is important to determine exactly how science will be taught.

Participants

The planning committee for construction, addition, or renovation of middle school facilities typically includes the principal, science teachers, teachers of nonscience subjects (if the school has an integrated curriculum), representative parents and students, the science supervisor, and the superintendent or assistant superintendent. In addition, the following groups may be represented on the committee or involved in various aspects of planning:
- science specialists
- science facilities specialists
- school administrators
- a university-based consultant
- school support services personnel
- architects
- furniture consultants
- community members

- business leaders.

If the project requires specific votes or approvals by the local government, consult with appropriate officials and political leaders from the start. Include custodians and facilities maintenance staff in discussions; they have a stake in the final product and can contribute practical suggestions to ensure that the facilities can be kept in good working order long after the project is completed.

Bring special education staff members and parents of special education students into the process for their expertise in identifying accessibility issues. The district or municipality should have a specialist knowledgeable about the Americans With Disabilities Act (ADA) requirements. Consult with this person, because he or she can offer suggestions on accessibility and advise architects of methods of compliance.

Preparation

Prior to beginning their work with designers, architects, and engineers, teachers and supervisors who will serve on the planning committee should try to acquire a background in understanding
- how the design and construction process works
- what factors affect construction costs
- how to read plans and specifications.

A subcommittee could be formed to gather input from the community and raise community awareness. The committee could develop a questionnaire and administer it to a group of students, educators, parents, and community representatives. The questionnaire should address areas of exemplary and safe science instruction as presented by the National Science Education Standards, the middle school science curriculum, and state and local regulations.

Planning

The planning committee should prepare a statement of needs and educational specifications that will provide the foundation for design and development. Checklists are useful at this stage to help ensure that various building, design, funding eligibility, space, equipment, and safety requirements are met.

Determine enrollment projections for short-term, mid-term, and long-term needs. If a population surge is anticipated, determine whether the bulge can be accommodated on a temporary (5- to 10-year) basis; if so, plan facilities that allow for low-cost modification for other uses in future years. For new construction or major renovations, a 20-year projection of needs should be developed.

An important consideration in planning school facilities is the movement to interdisciplinary teaming at the middle school level. It is critical to keep teaming in mind when planning middle school facilities so that science teachers do not have to use substandard facilities in order to keep student clusters intact.

Planning and design considerations include the following:
- the nature of the sciences taught and the overall educational program
- desired characteristics of the science facilities
- number of science facilities needed
- clustering of facilities
- safety requirements
- furnishings and equipment
- proposed computer use and other technology needs
- outdoor education areas
- adaptations for students with disabilities
- government regulations
- maintenance requirements
- budget
- time line.

Budget Priorities

The maxim "pay now or pay more later" applies here. A foundation for academic excellence begins with excellent facilities, which are not a luxury, but a requirement for maximum student achievement.

Space and safety are primary considerations in the planning budget. Lack of adequate space is much more costly to address later than the purchase of additional equipment, furniture, or new technology; also, overcrowding risks accidents and litigation. Any safety hazards resulting from poorly designed facilities will likely cause problems for the life of the building. In addition, good planning dictates that wiring and other accommodations for electronic equipment take into account both current and future needs.

In general, the cost of building and equipping a stand-alone student laboratory is twice that of a regular classroom, while the cost of a combination classroom/laboratory lies between the two. For all science facilities, annual budgets need to support operating costs, equipment maintenance and acquisition, and supplies.

Space Considerations

Space is an important factor in promoting inquiry, collaborative learning, and safety. Considering current technology needs and teaching practices, a good science room will require

- a minimum of 60 square feet* per student (5.6 square meters), which is equivalent to 1440 square feet (134 square meters) to accommodate a class of 24 safely in a combination laboratory/classroom—or—a minimum of 45 square feet per student (4.2 square meters), which is equivalent to 1,080 square feet (101 square meters) to accommodate a class of 24 safely in a stand-alone laboratory (The 1990 NSTA Position Statement on Laboratory Science recommends a maximum class size of 24 students in middle school).
- additional space to accommodate students with disabilities.
- 15 square feet (1.4 square meters) for each computer station with monitor, keyboard, CPU, printer, and CD-ROM.

* Measurements used by the trade are in feet and inches. European measurements are in meters and centimeters.

- 12 square feet (1.1 square meters) for a multimedia projector or data projector with a hard drive.

Adequate space is needed in or adjacent to the classroom for longer-term student projects. In addition, 10 square feet (0.9 square meters) per student is needed for teacher preparation space and for separate storage space (240 square feet, or 22 square meters, for a class of 24). Most science programs require a separate closet or room for storage of chemicals.

General Room Design

The design of an effective science room accommodates work in all science disciplines, with flexibility in furniture arrangement, abundant storage, sufficient working space for the safe conduct of activities, and holding space for ongoing projects. A rectangular room that is closer to being square works better than a long, narrow one. The room must have at least two exits and unobstructed doorways wide enough to accommodate students with physical disabilities. A ceiling height of 10 feet (3 meters) is desirable. Adequate ventilation (a minimum of 4 air changes per hour) is also important.

In addition to furnishings, equipment, wiring, and ventilation (discussed below), additional factors to consider are space for teacher planning, a view of the outdoors, daylight exposure (preferably southern) for plant growth, and the inclusion of a projecting plant window. Heating and cooling systems are necessary for year round use of facilities. Utilities such as gas, vacuum, compressed air, and waste handling systems should be provided as determined by the program's needs.

Furnishings for the Laboratory/Classroom

A laboratory/classroom with movable tables and perimeter counters, sinks, and utilities provides maximum flexibility in the use of space. Fixed lab stations or service islands require more space, and sight lines may not be as good. If the room has fixed lab stations, students should enter the room primarily by the door in the classroom area.

At the middle-school level, it is preferable that students not be seated at lab stations for long when not engaged in lab activities.

Sinks and work space

A large, deep sink with hot and cold water and 6 linear feet (1.8 meters) of adjacent counter space is needed for various purposes, such as cleaning large containers. Students' science investigations and cleanup require five or six sinks with water outlets along perimeter countertops or peninsulas. The sinks should be at least 18 inches (46 centimeters) in each dimension. Some means of acid dilution is needed. Depending on the science program, EPA regulations may require an acid-neutralization system.

Each student will need at least 6 linear feet (1.8 meters) of horizontal work surface. Sturdy, movable two-student laboratory tables, at least 54 inches (137 centimeters) long, are needed. (Flat-topped desks or tablet arm chairs are sufficient for lecture space in a room with fixed lab stations.)

Countertops 32 to 36 inches (81 to 91 centimeters) above the floor and tables 23 to 25 inches (58 to 64 centimeters) high are convenient for most middle school students. Chairs of a variety of seat heights can accommodate students of various heights. A counter depth of 30 inches (76 centimeters) is desirable. Ideally, all countertops and other top surfaces in classrooms, preparation rooms, and storerooms will have chemical-resistant finishes. Chemical-resistant synthetic stone or epoxy resin is recommended for countertops and lab table tops.

Storage and wall space

Provide base cabinets topped with counters along at least two walls for additional work and preparation space. All upper shelves and wall cabinets should be placed above base cabinets for safety reasons. Avoid particleboard assembly for casework unless a special sealant is used, because it is prone to problems with water penetration.

Chalkboards or marker boards and tackable wall surfaces for maps and posters are also needed; allot space for apron storage, safety shower, and eye wash; and plan floor space for a demonstration table and equipment such as laboratory carts, animal or plant study center, and stream table.

For specialized storage, include a storage closet (preferably at least 6 feet by 8 feet, or 1.8 by 2.4 meters); shelves and cabinets of various sizes for science equipment such as skeletons, torsos, and microscopes; and at least 36 linear feet (11 meters) of bookshelves. Make sure enough lockable cabinets are available for teacher use and for storing student projects. Wide, shallow drawers are useful for storing posters. Tall cabinets can be used to store tote trays for individual students' supplies and kits.

Shelving at least 10 inches (25 centimeters) deep for books and 15 to 18 inches (38 to 46 centimeters) deep for equipment should be provided, mounted on standards that allow adjustment to different heights. In general, shelving 12 inches (30 centimeters) deep is preferred for chemistry needs, 18 inches (46 centimeters) for biological equipment, and 24 inches (61 centimeters) for physical science equipment. Chemicals and potentially dangerous instruments should be kept in locked storage in a separate preparation or resource room and not in the classroom.

Ceiling hooks are useful for hanging demonstration and experimental apparatus. Rails may be used under lab table tops to hold tote trays, books, and papers. It is important to provide storage for students' coats and book bags in the room or nearby to keep these items out of the way during lab work.

A pull-down audiovisual screen may be mounted at an angle in a front corner of the room, so that its use does not block the view of the chalkboard.

Lighting and wiring

At least 8 covered, duplex electrical outlets with ground-fault-interrupter protection are needed at countertop height for the work spaces near the sinks, and additional outlets with ground-fault protection should be spaced frequently along the other walls for convenient use.

Provide wall outlets or recessed electrical floor boxes for computers and other equipment, as needed. Computers require separate circuits with surge protection and grounding. Also provide data connections to the school's computer network (or conduit and outlets for future connection) and wiring for voice, data, and video communications, as desired. A telephone or other provision for emergency help should be available in the science room or nearby.

The emergency shut-off controls for water, electrical service, and gas (if used) should be near the teacher's station, not far from the door, and not easily accessible to students. Master controls may include electric solenoid with key reactivation. The teacher's station should also have controls for room darkening and, if applicable, projection or video, computer imagery, and laserdisc media.

Lighting of a minimum of 50 foot-candles per square foot of floor surface (and 75 to 100 foot-candles at the work surface) is needed, as well as an emergency light (if adequate natural light is not available) in case of electricity failure. Room-darkening shades with edge tracks are necessary for various science activities. Dimming can be accomplished by using three-tube fluorescent lighting separately switched, so that one, two, or three tubes can be on at a time. Consider fluorescent lighting with parabolic lenses to reduce the glare on computer screens.

Equipment and Supplies

Most programs require a source of heat, such as gas or hot plates, for the students and teacher. Computers and appropriate software,

television monitor, VCR, videodisc player, a CD-ROM player, and an overhead projector (4,000 lumen for optimum use) are needed, as well as science materials and equipment including magnets, thermometers, hand lenses, microscopes, two-pan balances, measuring tools, models, plastic beakers, glass tubing, and containers. Laboratory carts with raised edges are required for the safe transport of materials. A projector for computer and video images is also recommended. Laptop computers with probeware, word-processing, and database software are desirable for use in field and outdoor studies as well as in the laboratory.

The following laboratory and field equipment is strongly recommended (as appropriate to the program):
- a clock with a sweep second hand
- overhead mirror above the demonstration table
- aquariums, terraria, and vivaria
- animal cages or study center
- incubator
- binocular or stereomicroscopes
- supply carts
- maps and globes
- astronomy equipment
- weather instruments
- stream table
- photography equipment
- microslide viewers
- videomicroscope
- tripod magnifiers
- germination/growth chamber
- refrigerator and dishwasher.

Make arrangements to ensure adequate year round care of animals, including backup heating systems and cooling systems for vacation periods.

Preparation and Storage Rooms

Ideally, a preparation room should be adjacent to the science room and near the storage areas. Consider providing a view window between the preparation and science rooms to facilitate supervision of students. Adequate

ventilation and safety equipment are required. A large, deep sink with a rubber mat, hot and cold water, and 4 linear feet (1.2 meters) of adjacent counter space are needed for preparation for safety reasons. Also provide the following:
- two duplex electrical outlets with ground-fault protection
- gas cock or hot plate
- a variety of shelves and cabinets
- 9 linear feet (2.7 meters) of bookshelves.

If a microwave oven is needed for demonstrations, it is best located in the preparation room. A refrigerator and dishwasher may be installed beneath a counter, and space may be allotted for other equipment, lab carts, and storage of glass tubing. A lowered section of countertop, 34 inches (86 centimeters) high, with knee space and drawers and with voice, data, and power outlets can serve as an office area for the teacher. Chemicals should not be stored in the preparation room, but should be kept in a separate, secure, and ventilated storage closet. State regulations must be observed.

Storage rooms supplement the storage areas in science rooms and provide needed security and specialized storage for large, expensive, or sensitive equipment.

A dedicated, locked chemical storage area that is well ventilated (12 air changes per hour forced-air ventilation) should be provided. Separation of incompatible materials is important, as are special precautions for flammable materials. When chemicals are stored, care should be taken that those that react with each other are not stored together. Design shelves to inhibit spread of spills, and use wood or other corrosion-resistant materials for the shelves and any attachments. It is desirable to limit shelf depth to 12 inches (30 centimeters) to prevent the storage of bottles behind one another. It is a good idea to install a lip edge on any open shelves used for storing bottles or chemicals. Chemicals should not be stored in the same room with equipment or master shut-off controls because the chemicals could corrode metal parts.

Safety Considerations

For safety reasons, adequate circulation space and strict observation of the limit on class size are important. For the students' protection, enclose any utilities lines that are above or below service islands.

The science room should have splash-proof safety goggles for all students and a goggles sanitizer. Providing one sink with soap dispenser for every four or five students also improves safety in the laboratory. In earthquake zones, doors or barriers should be secured to prevent spills caused by tremors. Chemistry and some physical science rooms must have exhaust fume hoods. Chemicals should never be stored in the classroom area.

In general, each laboratory and preparation room should have a centrally located
- safety shower and drain with a dual eyewash that provides a tempered flow of fresh aerated water for at least 15 minutes
- physician-approved first-aid kit
- fire blanket.

For maximum safety, all laboratory, preparation, and storage rooms should have
- at least two locking entrances
- adequate ventilation
- a chemical spill control kit
- an ABC fire extinguisher at each exit
- smoke/heat detectors.

Exhaust openings must be ventilated away from air intake openings. Fume hoods cannot replace the forced-air floor-to-ceiling ventilation necessary in science rooms.

Separate student project rooms also require safety equipment and well-marked exits.

An inventory of all chemicals should be kept in the main office and filed annually with the local fire chief.

Finally, be sure to provide supervision for custodians who clean chemical storage areas unless they have had specific training.

Earthquake Precautions

Recommendations and requirements for earthquake and hurricane precautions for school facilities can be obtained from the state disaster department.

Because books and equipment will fall off open shelves during earthquakes, cabinets with hinged doors and positive latches are recommended in areas subject to seismic activity. These cabinets should be bolted to walls and partitions. Deep tracks will help prevent sliding cabinet doors from being jolted out of their tracks by the upward motion of an earthquake. Lips or rods can help keep items from sliding off shelves; ideally, shelving for chemical storage will have individual recesses for each container.

It is advisable to clamp or bolt equipment to counters wherever possible. If computers are mounted on carts, the carts should be kept in cabinets when not in use. Major building codes specify requirements for walls, ceilings, and equipment.

Adaptations for Students with Disabilities

To accommodate students with physical disabilities, additional space is needed for specialized equipment, such as wheelchairs, and for aides who may accompany the student. An appropriate work area requires approximately twice the usual amount of space, that is, the equivalent of two work stations per student. Specialized equipment and furniture are also needed.

If each room has sufficient space, portable equipment and adjustable furniture can be used to make at least one work station in every room accessible to students with disabilities. Provision of adequate space requires significantly less expense than the installation of permanent equipment, which often goes unused.

Ways to ensure accessibility include
• providing braille equivalents on labels for switches and equipment
• using wire pulls on cabinets and lever-controlled faucets on sinks
• equipping emergency eyewashes with extendable hoses.

All wall-mounted objects should be above base cabinets so blind students will not risk bumping into them.

The *ADA Accessibility Guidelines for Buildings and Facilities* (ADAAG) defines a number of requirements for maximum counter heights, reach ranges, and grasping and twisting limitations. For example, the ADAAG specifies that sinks used by disabled students must be no more than 6 1/2 inches (17 centimeters) deep and must be mounted to accommodate students in wheelchairs. (For adults, this would mean a counter no more than 34 inches, or 86 centimeters, high, with 27 inches, or 69 centimeters, minimum vertical knee space.)

The school district advisor should have information about local, state, and federal guidelines. The ADA, enforced through the United States Department of Justice, requires compliance with ADAAG or *Uniform Federal Accessibility Standards* (UFAS) requirements.

Other Teaching Environments

Technology labs can offer computer simulation technology, which is used in both science and technology programs. A seminar room equipped with a computer work station and electronic communications system for electronic presentations is useful for small-group work and can be shared with other departments. A planetarium is recommended for the school district.

An optimal science program includes access to natural settings in which to study basic science concepts. (Be sure to include the outdoor areas for science activities in the initial facilities design plan.) The following are all desirable:
• native plants on the school grounds
• a garden
• a greenhouse with water source

- a storage shed for garden tools
- nature trails
- natural outdoor areas with a variety of environments
- educational kiosks.

A less expensive alternative to a greenhouse is a small (4 feet deep by 8 feet wide, or 1.2 by 2.4 meters) lean-to structure protruding from the wall of a science room, glazed with insulating glass, and equipped with supplementary day and night lighting and a floor drain.

"Designing Middle School Facilities" was written by James T. Biehle, Inside/Out Architecture, Inc., Clayton, Missouri; LaMoine L. Motz, Oakland County Schools, Waterford, Michigan; and Sandra S. West, Department of Biology, Southwest Texas State University, San Marcos.

Other contributors were Patricia S. Bowers, Center for Mathematics and Science, University of North Carolina, Chapel Hill; Terry Kwan, TK Associates, Brookline, Massachusetts; and Victor M. Showalter, Purdue University, West Lafayette, Indiana. Editor: Suzanne Lieblich.

RESOURCES FOR THE ROAD   Facilities

ADA Accessibility Guidelines for Buildings and Facilities. (Revised 1994). *Federal Register,* 28 CFR Part 36 (467).

American Association for the Advancement of Science (1991). *Barrier Free in Brief: Laboratories and Classrooms in Science and Engineering.* Washington, DC: Author.

American Chemical Society. (1995). *Safety in Academic Chemistry Laboratories* (6th ed.). Washington, DC: Author.

Biehle, James T. (1995, November). Six Science Labs for the 21st Century. *School Planning and Management,* 34 (9), 39–42.

Biehle, James T. (1995, May). Complying with Science. *American School and University,* 67 (9), 54–56. (Discusses ADA issues in science labs.)

California Department of Education, Science and Environmental Education

Unit. (1993). *Science Facilities Design for California Public Schools.* Sacramento, CA: Author.

Flinn Biological Catalog/Reference Manual. (1996). Batavia, IL: Flinn Scientific, Inc. (P.O. Box 219, Batavia, IL 60510; contains advice on safety in the laboratory.)

Flinn Chemical Catalog/Reference Manual. (1996). Batavia, IL: Flinn Scientific, Inc. (Contains advice on safety in the laboratory.)

Florida Department of Education. (1993). *Science for All Students: The Florida Pre K–12 Science Curriculum Framework.* Tallahassee, FL: Author.

Florida Department of Education. (1992). *Science Safety: No Game of Chance!* Tallahassee, FL: Author.

Governor's Committee on High School Science Laboratories for the 21st Century. (1992). *Look of the*

Future: Report of the Governor's Committee on High School Science Laboratories for the 21st Century. Baltimore, MD: State of Maryland, Public School Construction Program.

Kaufman, James A. *The Kaufman Letter* (quarterly newsletter on safety issues). Natick, MA: James A. Kaufman & Associates. (192 Worcester Road, Natick, MA 01760-2252.)

Los Angeles, Orange, and San Diego County Offices of Education. (1989). *Remodeling and Building Science Instruction Facilities in Elementary, Middle, Junior, and Senior High Schools.* (1989). Downey, CA: Los Angeles County Office of Education. (Also available from Orange County Department of Education, Costa Mesa, CA, and San Diego County Office of Education, San Diego, CA.)

Madrazo, Gerry M., Jr., and **Motz,** LaMoine L. (Eds.). (1993). *Fourth Sourcebook for Science Supervisors.* Arlington, VA: National Science Teachers Association.

Mione, Lawrence V. (1995). *Facilities Standards for Technology in New Jersey Schools.* Trenton, NJ: New Jersey State Department of Education.

National Science Teachers Association. (1995). Laboratory Science (Position statement). In *NSTA Handbook 1995–6* (pp. 209–212). Arlington, VA: Author.

National Science Teachers Association. (1993). *Safety in the Elementary Science Classroom* (Rev. ed.). Arlington, VA: Author.

Public Schools of North Carolina. (1991). *North Carolina Public Schools Facility Standards: A Guide for Planning School Facilities.* Raleigh, NC: North Carolina Department of Public Instruction, School Planning.

Public Schools of North Carolina. (1992). *Furnishing and Equipment Standards: A Guide for Planning and Equip-ping New Facilities and Evaluating Existing Schools.* Raleigh, NC: North Carolina Department of Public Instruction, School Planning.

Reese, Kenneth M. (Ed.). (1985). *Teaching Chemistry to Physically Handicapped Students* (Rev. ed.). Washington, DC: American Chemical Society.

School Facilities Branch, Maryland State Department of Education. (1994). *Science Facilities Design Guidelines.* Baltimore, MD: Author.

Showalter, Victor M. (Ed.). (1984). *Conditions for Good Science Teaching.* Arlington, VA: National Science Teachers Association.

Six Secrets to Holding a Good Meeting Every Time [Brochure]. (n.d.). Saint Paul, MN: 3M Company, Audiovisual Division.

Texas Education Agency (TEA). (1989). *Planning a Safe and Effective Science Learning Environment.* Austin, TX: Author. (Available from Publications, Distribution, and Fees Office, TEA, 1701 North Congress Avenue, Austin, TX 78701-1494.)

19 Texas Administrative Code, Chapter 61, Subchapter H (School Facilities Standards), '61.102. (Available from Director, School Facilities, TEA, 1701 North Congress Avenue, Austin, TX 78701-1494.)

Wang, Denis. (1994, February). A Working Laboratory. *The Science Teacher, 61* (2), 26–29.

Ward, John. (1992, September). Shopping for Science. *The Science Teacher, 59* (6), 28–33.

Ward, Susan, and **West, Sandra S.** (1990, May). Accidents in Texas High School Chemistry Labs. *The Texas Science Teacher, 19* (2), 14–19.

West, Sandra.S. (1991, September). Lab Safety. *The Science Teacher, 58* (6), 45–49.

Young, J.R. (1972). A Second Survey of Safety in Illinois High School Laboratories. *Journal of Chemical Education, 49* (1), 55. (Contains research on space necessary for science safety in the laboratory.)

Appendix D
Addresses for Program Information

AAAS/Project 2061
c/o Oxford University Press
198 Madison Ave.
New York, NY 10016-4314
(800) 451-7556
Benchmarks for Science Literacy

AIMS Education Foundation
P.O. Box 8120
Fresno, CA 93747-8120
(209) 255-4094
(888) 733-2467

American Chemical Society,
   Office of Prehigh School
1155 16th St., NW
Washington, DC 20036
(202) 452-6366
WonderScience Magazine

Biological Sciences Curriculum Study
   (BSCS)
5415 Mark Dabling Blvd.
Colorado Springs, CO 80918-3842
(719) 531-5550
cmonson@cc.colorado.edu
Making Healthy Decisions
Middle School Science & Technology

Curriculum Research & Development
   Group
University of Hawaii
1776 University Ave.
Honolulu, HI 96822
(800) 799-8111
crdg@hawaii.edu
Foundational Approaches in Science
   Teaching:
   FAST 1, The Local Environment
   FAST 2, Matter & Energy in the
   Biosphere
   FAST 3, Change Over Time

Lawrence Hall of Science
University of California at Berkeley
Berkeley, CA 94720-5200

   Chemicals, Health, Environment,
      and Me (CHEM)
   (510) 642-8718
   lhsinfo@uclink.berkley.edu

   Great Explorations in Math and
      Science (GEMS)
   (510) 642-7771
   gems@uclink.berkeley.edu

   Science Education for Public
      Understanding Program (SEPUP)
   (510) 642-8718
   sepup@uclink.berkeley.edu

NOTES

NOTES

NOTES

NOTES